Also by Kenneth M. Valentine

*Cheating Death: Three-Time Presidential Secret
Service Agent Lives to Tell You How*

STAYING SHARP

THE SUPPORT & CHALLENGE DEVOTIONAL FOR *CHEATING DEATH*

KENNETH M. VALENTINE

Liberatio
Protocol

A LIBERATIO PROTOCOL BOOK
An Imprint of Post Hill Press
ISBN: 979-8-88845-725-2
ISBN (eBook): 979-8-88845-726-9

Staying Sharp:
The Support & Challenge Devotional for Cheating Death
© 2025 by Kenneth M. Valentine
All Rights Reserved

Cover Design by Conroy Accord

This is a work of nonfiction. All people, locations, events, and situations are portrayed to the best of the author's memory.

This book, as well as any other Liberatio Protocol publications, may be purchased in bulk quantities at a special discounted rate. Contact orders@posthillpress.com for more information.

Post Hill Press
New York • Nashville
posthillpress.com

Published in the United States of America
1 2 3 4 5 6 7 8 9 10

Contents

Soul Support

High-Octane Challenge

Cover and Dedication

The cover of this book was inspired by a painting my daughter created for her fine arts degree, senior project, at the University of Oklahoma. Appreciating the work, the theme, and the color so much, I asked Sarah to work with me on this cover to incorporate the idea that staying sharp, for me, involves getting up early and engaging the Lord through Scripture and prayer (with coffee!). She nailed it!

Fittingly, I would like to dedicate this book to the three closest women in my life who provide wonderfully balanced support and challenge. To my wife, Sandra, and daughters Sarah Shelby and Georgia Grace: Thank you for your loving support and your gracious challenge.

Author proceeds from Staying Sharp will go to support The WellHouse (www.The-WellHouse.org), a home for victims of human sex trafficking. The WellHouse is a safe haven for female victims of human trafficking. Their mission statement is simple: "We exist to honor God by rescuing and providing opportunities for restoration to female victims of human trafficking who have been sexually exploited." Thank you for helping support this wonderful ministry. KV

**Two are better than one, because they
have a good reward for their toil.**

ECCLESIASTES 4:9

**I have no greater joy than to hear that my
children are walking in the truth.**

3 JOHN 4

Foreword

I am honored to write a few words about a man who I admire, and about a book that I have found to be encouraging and challenging. From the time I was introduced to Kenneth Valentine to this day, I have found him to be a leader who is focused on God, family, and serving others. We first met in a board meeting where we were considering a partnership. I learned very quickly the board had more to gain by him partnering with us than he did by joining our board. Our friendship has grown beyond partnering on boards and includes regular times of mentoring and encouragement over a meal, and him speaking to my congregation in my absence. I take neither lightly, but it takes much trust for a pastor to have someone speak while he is absent. He is a great blessing and is greatly concerned with rightly conveying God's Word in speech and in writing.

Ken asked me to read a draft of his book titled *Cheating Death* a couple years ago, and I found it to be one of my favorite reads. As a result, when I was asked to read *Staying Sharp* and to write the Foreword, I was honored. I found this book to be a strong and supporting follow-up to the first book. Ken provides supporting text from God's Word to express his foundation for faith and offers challenging text to help believers press toward the prize that awaits. This devotion will help followers of Christ grow in maturity and will provide encouragement when challenges arise. Ken's interpretation of the text is accurate, and his application of the text is spot-on.

I encourage every believer to read this devotional with an expectation of learning and growing in Christ. Consider offering this book to unbelievers to help them understand why we have hope within. May God bless you as you read this book, and may you draw closer to Him. May God bless Ken for the hard work and dedication he has shown in providing this encouraging and challenging devotion. Ken, I thank God for you and what you are doing for His kingdom.

Your friend and partner in Christ,
Dr. Jason Jarvis
Pastor & Leadership Consultant

Introduction

If you are like me, the day begins in one of several ways. Depending on the season of life, your day may begin with a workout, your devotion, hustling off to work, or preparing children for their day. Some of you may be doing all of this! Hopefully, all of you include a time for prayer and seeking the Lord on the front end of your day. There is something special that happens early in the morning. I have learned to appreciate the few extra minutes alone with the Lord, first thing in the morning.

Most of us, however, do not awaken in a strange place dealing with the horrors of being a sex trafficked human. I serve on the board of directors at both the National Center for Missing & Exploited Children, and The WellHouse. The WellHouse is a therapeutic home in Alabama for restoring the lives of women and girls who have been trafficked and sexually abused. Proceeds from this devotional will go to help support the ministry of The WellHouse. Imagine, with all you have to do getting ready for your day tomorrow, you add in the need to remind yourself that you are in a safe place, being cared for by people who love you sacrificially, that your traffickers will not have access to you today, and that there may be hope for something other than the life you have known.

As sinners, living in a fallen world, we are all in need of a savior. Praise God for His sacrificial provision of His only son, Jesus Christ as our savior, redeemer, and friend.

> **"Jesus said to her, 'Everyone who drinks of this water will be thirsty again, but whoever drinks of the water that I will give him will never be thirsty again. The water that I will give him will become in him a spring of water welling up to eternal life.'"**
>
> JOHN 4:13-14

Getting Started

What kind of imagery is conjured up in your mind when you are encouraged to *stay sharp*? I can hear my dad telling me to *stay sharp*. He meant not only to literally keep my pocketknife sharpened but to do those things in life that maintain the infrastructure ensuring success. It meant paying attention to what was going on around me (especially riding my bike on the county road) and being responsive to adults. It meant cleaning up after myself ("The job is not done until the mess is cleaned up," he would say) and attiring myself well (sagging socks weren't cool—they were meant to come all the way up to your knees!). Those words carried the mantle of doing your very best, all the time.

My dad let me handle knives at an early age. I could not have my own knife until I was ten years old—that was The Rule. I learned to appreciate the value, usefulness, and dangers of knives along the way. I recall the feeling of pride and power walking away from my dad, on my tenth birthday, with *my own* pocket knife in my pocket—thrilling. Then I got into Boy Scouts.

Boy Scouts were expected to *"be prepared"* (the Scout motto), and that usually included having a good, sharp knife. Not everyone, however, had a sharpening stone (even fewer actually knew the right way to make use of a sharpening stone). My friends and I carried knives that inevitably became dull. But every year, at Boy Scout camp, we had access to Mr. Jim, aka "The Knife Sharpener."

Mr. Jim had a cabin at the camp with a window containing a foldout ledge. He would open the window and fold out the ledge so everyone knew Mr. Jim was *in*. During certain hours of the week, you could stand in line at his cabin window and wait for Mr. Jim to sharpen your knife. You could hand Mr. Jim a brand-new knife, or one that barely cut through butter, and he would safely (always in the approved Boy Scout manner) hand you back a knife that was as sharp as a razor blade. He kept a box of Band-Aids on his window ledge for the new guys who tested the sharpness of his product on themselves. There was always one....

My college roommate, Tom, introduced me to a whole new level of knives and sharpness. I detailed how sharp Tom's knives were in my first book, *Cheating Death*—he could shave with them. Tom was intentional about everything he pursued. By that, I mean he did it right, and he did it well. In school at Purdue, Tom got all As. He researched, practiced, and invested time into each of his many hobbies. I witnessed Tom, on a snarky challenge, hit a coffee can lid from seventy yards away, with a hunting bow. The small crowd of veteran bow shooting experts was dumbfounded. Tom acted like he did that all the time, because he did. And in about 1987, even with the very best in compound hunting bow technology (which Tom had), seventy yards was extraordinary.

Tom pursues excellence—my dad would say "sharpness"—in everything he does. And if I need to have a surgery performed tomorrow, I would want Tom to perform that surgery, because he hasn't changed. He keeps his knife sharp, his skills honed, and his awareness up—awareness of the latest in surgical techniques, awareness of anything and everything that will make him the best at what he does. That's what you might expect of a surgeon, right?

How sharp are you? We can't all be Tom. Or can we? I can be like Tom in doing my very best with what I have been given. My contention is that while we are not all going to be surgeons, we can all be exactly what God intended us to be, both personally and professionally. I believe we get closer to realizing our potential with support and challenge.

The Merger

In *Cheating Death*, I devoted a chapter (by the same name) to the concept of "Support and Challenge." The two concepts are certainly separate and distinct. However, I consider these principles to be intertwined for a single new concept: support and challenge. When the two are merged, you get the third concept. Like with marriage, the two become one.

Imagine a rocket. A strong rocket has the support necessary to escape the gravity of earth and make its way into the sky. Powerful engines and fuel support the rocket getting off the ground. Excellent. Now what? If that rocket has a mission beyond making a show at blastoff, it will need a guidance system. The guidance system is just as important if that rocket is going to be useful or successful getting to a destination. The rocket's guidance system is the challenge. Instead of allowing the rocket to go wherever it would randomly wander, the guidance system steers the rocket toward the goal.

Do you identify with the rocket? Do you feel like you are boosted, supported, and travelling at a high rate of speed—but without a guidance system? Maybe you feel more like the rocket still on the launch pad—the guidance system is all green, but you don't have the support to help get you moving.

If you expected the next sentence to say, "This book will help you blast off and acquire your target," you may be disappointed. This is not *that* book. This book will, however, point you to that book. The book you want is the Bible. The Bible, God's Word, Holy Scripture, is all of that and more. *That* book is the book of history and of the future. *That* book is the road map and guidance system. *That* book is the source of all power and wisdom for eternity.

This book takes passages from *that* book and helps you understand more about a relationship with the Author. This book is merely a snack. If you are truly hungry, feast on the whole of God's Word.

Support and challenge can come in many forms, from many sources. And although the term may be relatively new, the concept of having people in your life to support and challenge you is not new. Support means encouragement, inspiration, and irrational love. Challenge means accountability, discipline, and tough love. Some have pointed to growth, greater productivity, or advancement in their ability to lead as potential outcomes of the support and challenge merger. I would simply say support and challenge makes us sharper.

In *Cheating Death*, I went so far as to compare this idea of the support-challenge merger to a knife. Support represents one side of the blade, challenge the opposite side. Together they form the business end of a knife. The edge of the knife is where support meets challenge. When they are intentionally ground into each other, you get a knife edge. Knives are useful instruments. Whether you are working at home, cooking in the kitchen, or performing surgery, a knife—especially a sharp knife—is a wonderful tool. A sharp knife in the hands of an expert is an exceptionally useful tool.

First Up

The next section of this book is called "Soul Support." I have plucked fifty-two of my favorite passages from the Word of God and supplied my own experience, context, or words of encouragement to encourage you—to support you. Each of these short pickup reminders will give you a shot of inspiration. These passages will provide you with weekly reminders of how far, wide, high, and deep is the love of God for you.

The support I am describing is unapologetically Christian. I offer that potentially unnecessary clarification because I believe a stand should be taken so there is no room for misunderstanding. To the extent that I am able, I intend to glorify the Triune God of the Bible, and His Word, through this endeavor. To be very clear, God Himself is the only lawgiver and judge (James 4:12), but I believe He has endowed us with enough common sense to discern right from wrong. In our current age of vitriol, when churches are removing verses, chapters, and books from Scripture, and watering down what remains, I reaffirm my belief in the whole of Scripture. I also believe the Bible is the only inspired, infallible, and authoritative Word of God (2 Timothy 3:16, 2 Peter 1:21). There is only one God, eternally existing in three persons: God the Father, God the Son, and God the Holy Spirit (Matthew 28:19, John 15:26, 1 John 5:7). I further believe in the deity of Jesus Christ, His virgin birth, sinless life, miracles performed, vicarious and atoning death, bodily resurrection, ascension to Heaven where He sits at the right hand of the Father, and His future return to earth (Matthew 1:18–23, 16:16, 28:6–7, Luke 1:26–27, and Hebrews 4:15, among others).

You were fearfully and wonderfully made for a specific and glorious purpose. Then you were bought and paid for at an enormous price. Sometimes we just need to be reminded. We need a pick-me-up! The Lord has, and always will, provide. This is the support side of support and challenge. A Holy God provides support to His kids through His Word. When you need a word of encouragement and a helping of support, you can lean into any of these fifty-two passages for a soul-supporting message.

In *Cheating Death*, I suggested the following regarding the effort to get more support:

> *Surround yourself with positive people who will speak truth into your life, support you in your pursuits, and encourage you to do your very best.*

This book is an effort to support you. I endeavor to speak truth here and support you in your pursuit of Jesus Christ. There is no end to the love and favor God is prepared to pour out on His children. Lean into Jesus and enjoy a relationship with Him. When I need a reminder of who God is, how much He loves me, or simply a word suggesting that things are going to be alright, I will go to one of these passages. I hope you are well supported as you lean into Him. I believe you will be! The proof will be when you offer to be support to someone else.

And in This Corner

In contrast, the "High-Octane Challenge" chapter is fifty-two of my favorite passages that are more of a kick in the seat! These are hard-hitting passages that serve on the challenge side of support and challenge. If, instead of seeking reassurance or promises from the Lord, you need a strong word, a reminder of His commands, or a zinger—flip over to the "High-Octane Challenge" section and brace yourself. You will be lovingly and repeatedly challenged in ways only Scripture can provide. Here is what I wrote about challenge from *Cheating Death*:

> *Surround yourself with people who will challenge you*
> *with the truth, tough love, and wisdom.*

As with support, I would like to challenge you (and myself) to do more, love more, and be more like Jesus. God will provide. Along the way, we have to be willing to allow Him access to tough areas of our lives. You can listen all day long. At some point, preferably now, we need to also obey. These passages will make a huge difference in your sharpness as you embrace the message and put the words into action.

Get Ready

Other than the separation between the support and challenge sections, there is no order to the passages. The passages are, however, numbered so that you can refind them easily. My suggestion is that you read one of these passages over and over (from either "Soul Support" or "High-Octane Challenge") every day for seven days (yes, the same passage). Think through each verse in the passage. Consider reading the Scripture out loud, as a prayer.

Reading through Scripture is awesome. Slowing down to "taste spiritual reality" is better. That's a quote from Dr. Donald Whitney, author of numerous books and the website www.biblicalspirituality.org. Dr. Whitney recommends meditating on Scripture and letting the Bible "brew" in your mind. That's the idea behind the repetition and staying on the passage for a week. For most of us, the idea of meditation conjures up notions and images that we will tend to steer clear of when we can. Have no fear here. Most of us are meditating on God's Word already. When you memorize a passage, you meditate on that passage toward the commitment to memory. That's just one way to meditate.

Unlike worldly meditation, where the goal is the emptying of the mind through mental passivity (which I'm not sure is even possible), Christian meditation involves filling your mind. Christian meditation is the mental activity of feasting on the Word of God. Consider the following passages. These passages point us toward the right approach for time set aside to seek the Lord:

> **This Book of the Law shall not depart from your mouth, but you shall meditate on it day and night, so that you may be careful to do according to all that is written in it. For then you will make your way prosperous, and then you will have good success.**
>
> JOSHUA 1:8

Prosperity and success, according to the Lord (not to be confused with some sort of prosperity gospel, which is no gospel at all), follows being careful to do what is written in the Law. That obedience comes from reading, considering, praying over, and talking with the Lord about what is written in the Law—all forms of Christian meditation.

> **But his delight is in the law of the Lord, and on his law he meditates day and night.**
>
> PSALM 1:2

If you are starting to see a pattern, good! God's Word was meant to be stewed over and given reflective consideration.

> **But the one who looks into the perfect law, the law of liberty, and perseveres, being no hearer who forgets but a doer who acts, he will be blessed in his doing.**
>
> JAMES 1:25

God's blessing follows loving, obedient action—action in accordance with His Word.

> **Do not be conformed to this world, but be transformed by the renewal of your mind, that by testing you may discern what is the will of God, what is good and acceptable and perfect.**
>
> ROMANS 12:2

The world has its own agenda for your mind. God has a good, pleasing, and perfect will that you will be able to discern when you are transformed by the renewing of your mind, aligning your mind with the mind and will of God, and pursuing Scripture to the point that it flows in your thoughts and conversations.

Get Set

In the "Soul Support" and "High-Octane Challenge" sections, the following page, on the right side of each passage, is intentionally a blank space for you to take notes. Maybe you want to document what you are experiencing as you pray through the passage for a week. Date the notes you take and revisit them with updates (it helps me to come back with a different color of ink).

Unlike novels or other self-help type books, this book is more of a resource tool. Unlike a devotional book, there is no beginning or end. You get to make use of this how you see fit. You can certainly plow through, cover to cover. You can also take a "Soul Support" chapter or a "High-Octane Challenge" chapter and methodically go one-a-week (back and forth) and make a two-year study out of the book. The resource is there regardless of the purpose or current need.

My hope is that you would consider reading through and engaging the support passages and the challenge passages with someone, maybe even as a group. God's Word is perfectly capable of penetrating your soul whether you go it alone, or if you are reading as part of a group. However, I do believe there is a dynamic possible in a group that benefits participants. You may be that person to whom a new or struggling believer turns in a moment of great need.

God may be looking to use you, so be open to the possibility that you are going to give to a group more than you are going to get (and, of course, everyone who has been there knows that the one who gives the most ends up getting the most out of it). To be consistent, I have to tell you that I believe strongly in the need for other people in our lives as support and challenge. I encourage even the lone wolf, the introvert, to find one other person to share life, accountability, and joy with. Just be open—God will provide.

God is for you! God loves you, cares for you, made plans for you, and He provides for you. Wallow in the riches of His grace and enjoy diving into His Word.

The Bible is the real source of ultimate support and challenge because it contains the inerrant, infallible words of God. Through His Word we can get to know Him and learn of His plan for us. I would point you straight to the Bible, and only the Bible, for pure spiritual sustenance. What I have penned is more like a CliffsNotes with passages of the Bible. My hope is that you will follow the pointer straight to the source. Take these passages and commentary as needed, and I hope you will see the value in pursuing all of Scripture in your relationship with the Lord.

God knows not only how to sharpen us and prepare us but also how to use that sharpened knife for good. Watch doors open as opportunity comes to those who prepare. Getting and staying sharp through support and challenge will help prepare you for what God has planned for you.

Iron sharpens iron, and one man sharpens another.

PROVERBS 27:17

Support and challenge come from the people with whom we surround ourselves—those friends you allow into your inner circle. This is why choosing friends is so critical. We are intentionally bringing these people past our perimeters and close to our heart. Jesus is the Son of God, an original part of the Triune God. The Bible says He was with God in the beginning (John 1:2). Many times, the Bible also refers to Jesus as our friend. As such, you need to allow Him into your inner circle. He actually has a rightful place at the center of our lives. When we are getting this right, our life revolves around Him. Don't miss the connection. Jesus is also called "The Word" (John 1:1), and I believe the very best support and challenge is found in Him. Therefore, a relationship with Him is a must.

Get sharp. Stay sharp! And remember The Point:

For we are his workmanship, created in Christ Jesus for good works, which God prepared beforehand, that we should walk in them.

EPHESIANS 2:10

Blessings to you as you pursue Him through His Word!
Go!

Soul Support

**Therefore encourage one another and build
one another up, just as you are doing.**

1 THESSALONIANS 5:11

1

Remind Yourself

**But this I call to mind, and therefore I have hope: The steadfast
love of the Lord never ceases; his mercies never come to an end;
they are new every morning; great is your faithfulness. "The Lord
is my portion," says my soul, "therefore I will hope in him."**

LAMENTATIONS 3:21–24

Scripture consistently reminds us to water the seeds of God's faithfulness in our mind. God knows we will face struggles, hardships, and disappointments—all part of living in a fallen world, outside the Garden. God's faithfulness is steadfast. He has proven His faithfulness many times over. He suggests that we turn our focus away from what is troubling us and turn instead to Him.

I chose to memorize this passage several years ago. I was soon faced with serious troubles in a leadership role that made me question the foundational, organizational tenets of the outfit I was leading. I drew the sword of God's Word (with this passage) and continually reminded myself that God is faithful, merciful, and steadfast.

Do you need to remind yourself of these truths? Are you allowing negative circumstances and overwhelming thoughts to win the battle in your head? The Lord is your portion, meaning that He is all you need for all the battles. Put your hope in Him as you remind yourself of these truths.

1. *God's perfect love never stops.* Not even when we have screwed something up and think we don't deserve His love. He still loves you.
2. *His mercies never cease.* His mercies may change over time, and He may adapt them to see His will completed, but they will never cease. When we look for His mercy, we will find it. He has purposed every day for you—even today—complete with mercies just for you.
3. *God's faithfulness is great.* He is consistent in His pursuit of us, and He is faithful to supply everything we need for life and godliness (2 Peter 1:3).

This passage begins by reminding us to remind ourselves how great and faithful God is. Instead of asking for hope, remind yourself of these things and watch hope well up in you.

Remind yourself of these truths. The open page to the right is there for you to consider making your own list of God's faithful provisions for you in your life.

2

I See Hope

As a deer pants for flowing streams, so pants my soul for you, O God. My soul thirsts for God, for the living God. When shall I come and appear before God? My tears have been my food day and night, while they say to me all the day long, "Where is your God?" These things I remember, as I pour out my soul: how I would go with the throng and lead them in procession to the house of God with glad shouts and songs of praise, a multitude keeping festival. Why are you cast down, O my soul, and why are you in turmoil within me? Hope in God; for I shall again praise him, my salvation and my God. My soul is cast down within me; therefore I remember you from the land of Jordan and of Hermon, from Mount Mizar. Deep calls to deep at the roar of your waterfalls; all your breakers and your waves have gone over me. By day the Lord commands his steadfast love, and at night his song is with me, a prayer to the God of my life. I say to God, my rock: "Why have you forgotten me? Why do I go mourning because of the oppression of the enemy?" As with a deadly wound in my bones, my adversaries taunt me, while they say to me all the day long, "Where is your God?" Why are you cast down, O my soul, and why are you in turmoil within me? Hope in God; for I shall again praise him, my salvation and my God.

PSALM 42

The psalmist seems conflicted. At once he is both hungry for the Lord *and* bitterly depressed. God welcomes the honesty of His children. Acknowledge the truth to God, knowing He accepts you and cares about every detail of what you are feeling. Confess the downcast perspective. Ask Him for fresh perspective—His perspective. The psalmist recognized the downcast feelings, prayed over them in confession to God, and determined to remember God. He then calls out powerful truths about God. The psalmist ends his thoughts while still under attack but with renewed hope and a plan to praise God.

Are you being taunted and harassed by negative thoughts and depressing perspectives? Know that the Lord loves you in the midst of your storm. Confide in Him. Lift your gaze off your current entanglements and make a plan to praise the Lord. Consider writing down the things you choose to remember as you seek the Lord. Hope in the Lord! You will again praise Him!

3

Imago Dei

**So God created man in his own image, in the image of God
he created him; male and female he created them.**

GENESIS 1:27

**And God saw everything that he had made,
and behold, it was very good.**

GENESIS 1:31

Imago Dei is a Latin phrase meaning "image of God." You were fearfully and wonderfully made, in the image of God. We were made with God Himself as the prototype. God laid out all the facts about His creation and said it was "good." Then, after detailing the creation of people, all of a sudden He describes His creation as "very good"!

When was the last time you marveled at God's creation? Take in a sunrise or sunset, maybe a mountain view, or the still quiet over a pond in the middle of nowhere. All of these natural beauties are here for our appreciation and His glory. He even says His creation is good. And then He added people.... Have a look in the mirror. That image looking back at you in the mirror is made in the likeness of the Lord. Yes, we are sinful and even pathetic at times. We should be unlovable by a god who is perfect. Our God, however, called us "very good" from the beginning. Despite our rebellion, He sent His Son to pay the penalty for our sin—past, present, and future.

Remind yourself that you were made in the image and likeness of God Himself. He loved you from the beginning and provided the only solution to the problem of sin, through Jesus. His love for you continues to this day and will continue until He brings you home.

Consider making a list of things in creation that you appreciate. Give God thanks for His creation and for the gift of enjoyment. Add yourself to the list. Thank God for making you.

Of all His creation, only we have the ability to appreciate the rest of creation. Praise God for His outstanding work at creation.

4

Important Distinction

They shall be mine, says the Lord of hosts, in the day when I make up my treasured possession, and I will spare them as a man spares his son who serves him. Then once more you shall see the distinction between the righteous and the wicked, between one who serves God and one who does not serve him.

MALACHI 3:17–18

Malachi is the last book of the Old Testament and literally ends with the word "cursed." Four hundred silent years pass until our Savior appears, and the distinction referred to here by Malachi begins.

Read that passage again. Who do you think the "they" in the first line refers to? Do you feel like the "they" in "they shall be mine" must refer to someone, even anyone, besides you? You are likely in good company feeling this way. Feelings can be influenced and changed. Good feelings, bad feelings, right ones, and wrong ones all have this in common: they are subject to change, manipulation, reversal, and reinforcement. Feelings can be a wonderful part of the human experience. Feelings, however, can be fragile. Put your trust in facts over feelings.

God's Word, His love, and His individual plan for you are real, perfect, and good. You are His. He loves you completely, even if you aren't feeling it right now. You are His treasured possession, and He has an eternal plan to take care of you. You will see the plan unfold in your life as you abide in Him and seek Him. You will also see the divide between those who serve Him and those who choose not to serve Him.

Remind your feelings that God loves you, sacrificed His Son for you, and has great plans for you. Refix your gaze upon Him and see if the feelings follow.

5

Faithful Man

**When Joseph woke from sleep, he did as the angel of the Lord
commanded him: he took his wife, but knew her not until
she had given birth to a son. And he called his name Jesus.**

MATTHEW 1:24–25

Joseph gets overlooked a lot. He gets no talking lines in our Christmas shows, no songs about him, and few namesakes. Most people probably think of the Old Testament Joseph before thinking of Joseph, the faithful dad of Jesus. We don't know that much about him other than the limited mention he gets in Scripture. God could have chosen from many devout or faithful men. For the husband of Mary, and dad to the Savior of the world, however, God chose Joseph. We do know that Joseph was faithful. He did exactly what the angel of the Lord asked him to do.

What sticks out in your faith walk? Would your inner circle describe you as faithful? Does your inner voice recall more failures than successes? We don't have recorded stories of Joseph's failures, but he was prone to mistakes just like us. My guess is God chose Joseph because he was faithful in so many little things—thoughts, attitudes, and obedience when nobody was looking—knowing that Joseph would be faithful when called upon for the big acts of obedience.

Ask the Lord to remind you of some of your successes—even faithful acts that you think are of little consequence. Consider writing them down.

6

Moving Mountains

And Jesus answered them, "Have faith in God. Truly, I say to you, whoever says to this mountain, 'Be taken up and thrown into the sea,' and does not doubt in his heart, but believes that what he says will come to pass, it will be done for him. Therefore I tell you, whatever you ask in prayer, believe that you have received it, and it will be yours.

MARK 11:22–24

Is there a mountain in your way? A wall, barrier, or impediment that you cannot see through or around? Maybe Jesus just picked the most obvious visual object available to describe our ability through Him. Mountains? Whatever we ask for is ours for the asking? Immediately, the number of prayers for worldly possessions goes up! I will let you wrestle with God on that prayer (and see if He will provide a little something for me, too, if you are asking).

God initiated the relationship with you (Ephesians 2) and gave you the gift of faith. With a mountain in your path, Jesus says to "have faith in God." I believe He is asking you to use your gift—exercise your faith—and then watch the faithfulness of a loving Father work this out for His child. Jesus makes an incredible promise that often gets pushed aside in favor of more "reasonable and likely" promises. The mountain may be the hindrance to greater faith in God. Lean into Jesus for greater understanding.

Is the mountain in your way really a material issue? Is the possession or material issue part of the mountain? Consider making a list of the mountains you would like to see thrown into the sea. God wants an ever-deepening relationship with you. Are there hindrances there that should be cast into the sea as well? Have faith in God to see mountains in your life, or in your faith, removed. God can and will do this. Are you ready?

7

Ordinary Boldness

Now when they saw the boldness of Peter and John, and perceived that they were uneducated, common men, they were astonished. And they recognized that they had been with Jesus.

ACTS 4:13

This, for me, is one of the most striking passages in the New Testament. Jesus has been executed, come back to life, met with His disciples, and ascended back to Heaven. The disciples, much like us when our salvation is new, were out joyously telling the world about Jesus. They were preaching, and even healing people, in the name of Jesus. Arrest, jail, and threats could not quell the disciples' fervor. The authorities desperately wanted to shut these men up and stop the spread of the word about Jesus. To their astonishment, Peter and John were courageously proclaiming victory through a man, Jesus, whom they thought they had just dealt with through execution by the Roman government. Peter and John were unschooled, ordinary men who had been with Jesus.

Have you been with Jesus? If the answer is no, then today may be the day you get to change that answer to yes! The invitation to believe in Him, and trust Him as your Lord and Savior, may be upon you now.

If you have been with Jesus, consider documenting times when you walked closely with Him. Are you walking with Jesus now? Would you say you are walking closely? If not, pray to understand what has changed. Document answers as reminders. Do people see and know that you have been with Jesus?

God wants an ever-deepening relationship with you. Jesus offers to walk with you as you navigate and live this life for Him. He offers to walk so closely with you that people will be astonished, not at your possessions or uniqueness but because you walk with Jesus.

8

Rejoice Regardless

Therefore, since we have been justified by faith, we have peace with God through our Lord Jesus Christ. Through him we have also obtained access by faith into this grace in which we stand, and we rejoice in hope of the glory of God. Not only that, but we rejoice in our sufferings, knowing that suffering produces endurance, and endurance produces character, and character produces hope, and hope does not put us to shame, because God's love has been poured into our hearts through the Holy Spirit who has been given to us.

ROMANS 5:1–5

The "peace" that Paul talks of, in verse one, is ours in a relationship with God, through Jesus. Real peace with God does not exist outside a relationship with Jesus Christ. The peace contemplated in this passage is an eternal promise, an alignment with God, and it is ours forever because of, and through, Jesus. We are also simultaneously positioned in His grace, through faith. Peace and grace means we have His love, favor, protection, and hope—all in an eternal relationship. That is some wonderful, factual truth. Pause to give praise on that thought.

Real life is going to include real suffering. You can count on various hardships and have already experienced suffering, likely on many levels. You can also rejoice in the midst of your suffering. Are you enduring a painful issue, a hurt that won't stop, or a wrong with no sign of right? God has you in His grace. The peace is still there, even if circumstances have clouded our sunshine.

Rejoicing in our suffering is an act of faithfulness that we choose in light of the grace and peace we have been given through Jesus. Our suffering can produce despair, but it doesn't have to. Suffering can also produce hope. Along the way, as we lean into the Lord, suffering can also develop endurance and character.

Endurance and character, like patience or fitness, grows. It helps to lift our focus off the suffering, off the effort to endure, off the development of character. Lift your gaze to the Lord. As you focus on Him, rejoice!

"Holy Spirit, would you help me to endure the current suffering with peace. Thank you for the faith; thank you for hope; thank you for love. Help me to rejoice!"

Consider some notes on your suffering and on your prayer for peace and rejoicing in the midst of suffering.

9

You Are Blessed

And he lifted up his eyes on his disciples, and said: "Blessed are you who are poor, for yours is the kingdom of God. "Blessed are you who are hungry now, for you shall be satisfied. "Blessed are you who weep now, for you shall laugh. "Blessed are you when people hate you and when they exclude you and revile you and spurn your name as evil, on account of the Son of Man! Rejoice in that day, and leap for joy, for behold, your reward is great in heaven; for so their fathers did to the prophets.

LUKE 6:20–23

When was the last time you leaped for joy? Was it over a sporting event, a personal victory, or maybe you don't even recall the last time joy came out of you in such a visible, physical manner?

Jesus looked up to make eye contact with His disciples for a very important message: brace yourselves for what is coming. Jesus knew His followers would be poor, hungry, sorrowful, and despised—all because of their relationship with Him. Jesus is in the business of preparing and providing for His followers.

Know that the price we pay for following Jesus was foretold by Jesus Himself. But Jesus did not end with, "So hang in there," or, "Deal with it!" Our Lord provides hope in the midst of our troubles. These hopeful reminders can help us lift our gaze off the here and now and look ahead to what He has planned for us. God has yet to backtrack on a promise.

You have a reward waiting for you in Heaven with your name on it. These current issues will be long over and barely remembered. Consider writing down the promises from this passage and comparing that list to a list of troubles you are enduring in the name of Jesus.

Rejoice in the Lord! God's blessing and promises are upon you! Your reward is great in Heaven. Feel free to leap for joy.

10

Guaranteed

**Jesus said to them, "I am the bread of life; whoever comes to me
shall not hunger, and whoever believes in me shall never thirst.
But I said to you that you have seen me and yet do not believe. All
that the Father gives me will come to me, and whoever comes to
me I will never cast out. For I have come down from heaven, not
to do my own will but the will of him who sent me. And this is the
will of him who sent me, that I should lose nothing of all that he
has given me, but raise it up on the last day. For this is the will of
my Father, that everyone who looks on the Son and believes in him
should have eternal life, and I will raise him up on the last day."**

JOHN 6:35–40

Jesus continually offers Himself to us. He didn't just offer Himself as bread.
He offered Himself as the "bread of life," clearly portraying Himself as what
we all need for sustaining all manner of life. God knows exactly what we
need to live a life devoted to Him. Jesus offers Himself as the solution for
our every need. Whether your need is physical, spiritual, or mental—Jesus
is the provision. When His disciples wanted to feed a hungry crowd, Jesus
was the answer. Every need and want was brought to Jesus.

You were purchased at a high price. Just like any good investor, your
owner will make certain that He takes care of His investment. He will
continually supply everything you need to follow Him. Lean into Jesus.
Tell Him your needs, wants, and concerns. Talking to Him is part of your
growing relationship and reliance on the bread of life.

What are your needs this week? Consider writing these things down
and offer that list in a prayer. God loves you and cares about you. He cares
about your list. He has promised to raise you up on the last day. Between
now and the last day, trust Him to provide for all your needs.

11

Welcome Guest

"Let not your hearts be troubled. Believe in God; believe also in me. In my Father's house are many rooms. If it were not so, would I have told you that I go to prepare a place for you? And if I go and prepare a place for you, I will come again and will take you to myself, that where I am you may be also. And you know the way to where I am going."

JOHN 14:1–4

Is your heart troubled? Is it from something you did (or did not do), or something that was done to you? Can you even identify what is troubling you? You are not alone.

In this passage, Jesus has just washed His disciples' feet and sent Judas off in his betrayal. It is the last supper with Jesus, and the disciples can tell that something big is about to happen. They were likely anxious, and very concerned about Judas. Now Jesus is telling them that He is leaving, but somehow, they will know where He is going? Their hearts were troubled, and Jesus knew it.

His response to their troubles: Believe in Me. Replace the troubled thoughts, feelings, and notions about how things should be going or how they would be going if you were in charge. Instead, trust in the One who has promised to prepare a place for you. God is preparing that place for you right now. Jesus will come again and take you Home. In the meantime, don't settle on trouble. Settle on the Truth and make your plans for His return.

Consider making some notes about your own concerns right now. Can you identify with the concerns and worries of the disciples? If your heart is troubled, Jesus would like to deal with that. Let your heart troubles be substituted with belief in the One who loves you and is preparing a place for you right now.

12

More Than Conquer

...in all these things we are more than conquerors through him who loved us. For I am sure that neither death nor life, nor angels nor rulers, nor things present nor things to come, nor powers, nor height nor depth, nor anything else in all creation, will be able to separate us from the love of God in Christ Jesus our Lord.

ROMANS 8:37–39

Are you prepared to rise up and go beyond conquering for the Lord? The truthful answer from most of us is probably: "No, I don't feel like I am." I support you in your honesty. Theologically, you may even arguably be right to say no! How do we square the truth of Scripture claiming we are more than conquerors with where we are in reality—feeling like we are not even conquering, let alone more than conquering? Let's walk through this.

Think through your plan for being more than a conqueror—for overcoming all the horrible, worldly muck that tends to stick to us. If your plan has multiple steps, then I would pause and reconsider your plans. The only plan you need for conquering all the ills and evil in this world is to lean into Jesus. Jesus is the One who overcomes the world. We are invited to ride with Him as He accomplishes everything.

The love of God in Christ Jesus our Lord is the single most powerful force in existence. No matter where you go, or what you have done, you can open your eyes and find that the love of God is still there for you. No person, power, or circumstance can come between you and the Lord.

God sacrificed His own Son to permanently open the door and allow His love access to us. Nothing you can do, not do, or imagine can change that truth. All these things—hardships, failures, exposure, persecution, and trouble—are overcome through Him who loves us. Nothing can change that.

What do you need to write down in response?

Seven Promises

I give thanks to my God always for you because of the grace of God that was given you in Christ Jesus, that in every way you were enriched in him in all speech and all knowledge—even as the testimony about Christ was confirmed among you—so that you are not lacking in any gift, as you wait for the revealing of our Lord Jesus Christ, who will sustain you to the end, guiltless in the day of our Lord Jesus Christ. God is faithful, by whom you were called into the fellowship of his Son, Jesus Christ our Lord.

1 CORINTHIANS 1:4–9

Sometimes when we look down at the water, we only see our reflection staring back at us. How different the view is when we actually put our head into the water! Perspective is very important, and sometimes we need to look beyond the surface. The apostle Paul noted all these truths about being in a relationship with Christ, and it generates thanks. How many truths do you pull from this passage?

God's grace is poured out on you through Jesus Christ. In Him you lack nothing. You are enriched in knowledge and in speech. You will be sustained and found guiltless on the Day of Judgment. Yet again, God is called "faithful."

God is faithful. He loved you first. He pursues you for a relationship knowing everything about you, because He loves you. The testimony about Christ is confirmed in you. Praise God!

Consider making a list of promises and see how many you can memorize this week. Gratitude will overtake your heart and be available to spread to others. As the Lord sustains you by His grace, look for someone to encourage with the same message and thankfulness.

14

Comfort

**Blessed be the God and Father of our Lord Jesus Christ, the
Father of mercies and God of all comfort, who comforts us in
all our affliction, so that we may be able to comfort those who
are in any affliction, with the comfort with which we ourselves
are comforted by God. For as we share abundantly in Christ's
sufferings, so through Christ we share abundantly in comfort
too. If we are afflicted, it is for your comfort and salvation;
and if we are comforted, it is for your comfort, which you
experience when you patiently endure the same sufferings that
we suffer. Our hope for you is unshaken, for we know that as
you share in our sufferings, you will also share in our comfort.**

2 CORINTHIANS 1:3–7

Why do we pretend that everything is okay with us and then keep that
bottled up? Do we habitually deny that anything is going on with us? Give
the smile heading into church and acknowledge that everything is going
well with a hearty thumbs up, when in reality, things aren't always so great?
Why would anyone who is struggling ever admit their affliction in most of
our churches when they are surrounded by posers acting as if they have it
all figured out?

When we confess and admit our troubles, the doors open for God to
provide what we need for healing. God has this historic tendency to use
people. People who have received God's provision of comfort in times of
trouble can be a source of comfort to you. God is willing and able to provide comfort to you. He is the God of all comfort. Your thankful response
is to pray about with whom He will ask you to share that comfort.

Praise God! You know that He will provide you comfort, and it will be
so abundant that you will have leftovers to share with someone else.

Do you have a list of afflictions that you need to place at the foot of the
cross? Do you have a list of afflictions you have seen lifted from you that
deserve a "thank you"? How about a list of people you would like to comfort? If you are open, the Lord has a list He would like to share with you.

15

God Is Merciful

**The snares of death encompassed me; the pangs of Sheol
laid hold on me; I suffered distress and anguish. Then I called
on the name of the Lord: "O Lord, I pray, deliver my soul!"
Gracious is the Lord, and righteous; our God is merciful.**

PSALM 116:3–5

Can you relate to suffering distress and anguish? Have you felt as if death and utter darkness have laid hold on you, even encompassed you? Maybe you even wonder if anyone has ever endured what you are going through right now. You may even have succumbed to the notion that there is no clear path back to where you would like to be. Darkness seems to have engulfed the light, and the path is not visible to you.

The psalmist seems to capture the darkness and despair pretty well, with just a few words. Suffering can come in many forms, from physical pain and hurt, to emotional wounding and mental torture. If this is where you are right now, I am sorry you are suffering. I would encourage you to document your suffering. Acknowledge the pain and take some time to put parameters around what the suffering is, maybe even from where you believe your suffering came. First, however, I would call on the Name of the Lord. Let the Lord guide you as you identify your pain. Relate to the One who can actually identify with suffering and help you manage your issue(s).

God wants a deep relationship with you, and He may have allowed the suffering to teach you, help you grow, or simply to get your attention. Suffering can yield positive outcomes when we endure it with a right attitude. Call to the Lord. Praise Him in the midst of your distress.

The Lord is gracious. He is righteous. God is merciful. In your distress, turn, like the psalmist, to the One able to deliver you and restore you.

16

Power Prayer

For this reason I bow my knees before the Father, from whom every family in heaven and on earth is named, that according to the riches of his glory he may grant you to be strengthened with power through his Spirit in your inner being, so that Christ may dwell in your hearts through faith—that you, being rooted and grounded in love, may have strength to comprehend with all the saints what is the breadth and length and height and depth, and to know the love of Christ that surpasses knowledge, that you may be filled with all the fullness of God. Now to him who is able to do far more abundantly than all that we ask or think, according to the power at work within us, to him be glory in the church and in Christ Jesus throughout all generations, forever and ever. Amen.

EPHESIANS 3:14–21

Are you having a hard time adding an "amen" of agreement to the end of this passage? Are you not feeling the fullness of the Lord right now? There have been times when I have come across this passage and the sentences seemed to culminate in a loud crescendo, speeding up to an exuberant *amen*! (It helps that this whole passage is one long sentence.) Other times I have read this and not been quite so excited about it. What is going on with me? Can you relate?

Paul is on his knees in gratitude to the Lord for granting us all access to Him. Because of Jesus Christ, the Spirit is at work in you and me. He is strengthening our hearts for God with an amazing substructure. This infrastructure of faith is rooted and grounded in His perfect love for us. The work has all been overseen by a loving and generous Father. What more do I need to feel more exuberant (again) in my response to everything He has done for me?

When I have caught myself reading Scripture because I am supposed to be reading Scripture, I have learned to pause. God could have any part of His creation consume Scripture and coldly read it back to Him. I remind myself that He chose me (and you) for a relationship. When my approach is dry, I try reading the passage out loud (when possible) with a smile on my face (always possible). Focus on the truths offered by God through Paul's letter to the Ephesian believers. Maybe it would help to write out some of the truths from this passage.

Try reading this passage out loud as your own prayer to the Lord. He is able to do far more than what we imagine in our asking.

When your heart cries "amen" to the Lord, in agreement with Paul and in humble gratitude to your God, see with whom you can share your experience.

17

Confidence in Completion

I thank my God in all my remembrance of you, always in every prayer of mine for you all making my prayer with joy, because of your partnership in the gospel from the first day until now. And I am sure of this, that he who began a good work in you will bring it to completion at the day of Jesus Christ.

PHILIPPIANS 1:3–6

There are so many paths in life that I have not taken for a lack of vision. When I surveyed a particular path, if I could not see all the steps, I looked for a different path where I could see the steps. I would like to couch those decisions in a nice way—maybe as a lack of confidence or youthful uncertainty. Fear, however, is the real culprit—fear of failure, fear of embarrassment.

Regardless of our own vision, confidence level, or certainty, we can actually be certain of very little. There is always risk and uncertainty with the things of this world. We tend to fill the gap, or allow the gap to be filled, with fear when our focus is on the wrong things.

Enter Paul's prayer over the Philippian church. Paul reminds them of what they can be certain of in this life: that Jesus Christ began a good work in you, and He will be with you until the end.

For me, knowing the conclusion is guaranteed helps me with the here and now. I may not see the steps to the conclusion, so I have to be intentional about trusting in the One who does see the steps. Do you really believe God will let you flounder and fail, then show up for the last day? Jesus initiated this relationship because He loves you. He wanted you the day He created you, and He wants you in a relationship with Him every day until your completion in Jesus Christ.

Lean into Jesus today, regardless of what you see or feel. You can be sure that the good work started in you will be carried on to glorious completion at the day of Christ Jesus.

18

Rejoice and Pray

Rejoice in the Lord always; again I will say, rejoice. Let your reasonableness be known to everyone. The Lord is at hand; do not be anxious about anything, but in everything by prayer and supplication with thanksgiving let your requests be made known to God. And the peace of God, which surpasses all understanding, will guard your hearts and your minds in Christ Jesus.

PHILIPPIANS 4:4–7

This is an often-quoted verse by so many Christians, committed to memory as a reminder about not being anxious. Many times I have come across or turned to this verse and focused in on the "do not be anxious about anything" portion. This passage, however, contains four actions for you to do—commands, if you will—and the command to not be anxious is the third. Consider picking out the commands and writing them down. Pray over your current level of adherence to these.

I looked up various Bible versions regarding the second sentence: "Let your reasonableness be known to everyone." Other versions use "gentleness" or "graciousness" for "reasonableness." Only after telling us to rejoice in the Lord always, then saying it again, are we told to make sure our reasonableness is how we are known to everyone. And only after those two commands are we then reminded that the Lord is here with us, so let go of the anxiety. Instead of anxiety, we are told to pray and turn it all over to God, who is right there with us.

If I am obedient and spend my time rejoicing in the Lord—really being intentional about praising the Giver of every good gift, being disciplined in my effort to be gracious and gentle with everyone I meet, taking captive those anxious thoughts to make them obedient to Christ, and then prayerfully and thankfully spending time with the Lord (including my requests)—then I will be emptied of me and filled with Him. This is where I want to be.

19

God with You

Finally, brothers, whatever is true, whatever is honorable, whatever is just, whatever is pure, whatever is lovely, whatever is commendable, if there is any excellence, if there is anything worthy of praise, think about these things. What you have learned and received and heard and seen in me—practice these things, and the God of peace will be with you.

PHILIPPIANS 4:8–9

We have a tendency to drift.… We get distracted, focused on what we see and on what we want to do for the Lord. If you have ever operated a small boat with a little engine—one that you steer by pushing the motor grip left or right at the back of the boat—then you will appreciate how difficult it is to steer the boat looking back at the motor.

God's instruction tells us how to align ourselves with what He is doing in the world. When our minds are intentionally thinking about godly things, the ungodly things are displaced. Focus this day on what you know to be true. Appreciate honorable and just people and stories. Make time to recall what is pure, lovely, and commendable in God's creation. Things that are excellent and praiseworthy, think about these things. Make a list of these things and praise God for all He has done. Practice these things and see that the God of peace is with you.

20

Heart and Mind

If then you have been raised with Christ, seek the things that are above, where Christ is, seated at the right hand of God. Set your minds on things that are above, not on things that are on earth. For you have died, and your life is hidden with Christ in God.

COLOSSIANS 3:1–3

The central question for eternity is, "Have you been raised with Christ?"

If the answer is yes, this passage has some simple and direct guidance for you:

1. Seek the things that are above. Many times we are told to change our focus or lift our gaze to heavenly things. You will see that Christ is seated at the right hand of God. The second is like the first:
2. Set your mind on things that are above. This is in contrast to the earthly matters that we tend to stew over in our mind.

Consider a prayer of thanks to the Lord for His redemption of you, followed by confession of all your worldly distractions. Ask for help focusing on heavenly things. Praise God that because of Christ's redemptive work, your life is hidden in His. Be intentional this week about seeking His kingdom first.

If you are not sure that you are raised with Christ, make that uncertainty a prayer. Know, too, that salvation rests in, and through, Christ alone. We are saved through the gift of faith, not by our own efforts (please have a look at 1 John 5:13 and Ephesians 2:8–9).

Praise God for every good and perfect gift!

21

God's Will for You

**Rejoice always, pray without ceasing, give thanks in all
circumstances; for this is the will of God in Christ Jesus for you.**

1 THESSALONIANS 5:16–18

Are your current circumstances distracting you from Jesus? Is your prayer
life relegated to certain times of the day? Does the Lord hear from you only
when you are in need? Join me in confessing all these things!

God's will for you in Christ Jesus is so much more than a box to check
or a prayer to repeat. As an adopted child of God, you are a sibling of
Christ and sought-after for a family relationship.

When all your own might and effort are failing to bring about the peace
of God, know that you have sought Him *outside* of His will. In this passage,
Paul breaks down for us three practices for seeking Him *inside* His will:

1. *Rejoice always.* The attitude of gratitude will impact your heart
   and those around you. Consider writing down five things you can
   rejoice about this week. God's will is that you would start your day
   with rejoicing and continue the song throughout the day. There is
   no blackout period for us in rejoicing.
2. *Pray without ceasing.* God's will for us is a relationship. We relate
   through prayer and reading His Word. Prayer can continue as a
   relational conversation, regardless of where we are during the day.
3. *Give thanks in all circumstances.* Just in case we missed that part
   about rejoicing and praying, God takes away the exceptions we
   would allow ourselves.

God's will is not a secret. He has made His desire for us abundantly
clear. Is there anything distracting you from rejoicing, praying, and giving thanks to the Lord? God will likely want to hear what this is that you
believe is between Him and His beloved child. Talk to Him about these
things. Make notes to remind yourself. Then be intentional about return-
ing to this verse and centering yourself in God's will for you.

22

Looking Forward

I have fought the good fight, I have finished the race, I have kept the faith. Henceforth there is laid up for me the crown of righteousness, which the Lord, the righteous judge, will award to me on that day, and not only to me but also to all who have loved his appearing.

2 TIMOTHY 4:7–8

Are you weary from fighting battles everywhere you turn? Do you ever feel like you are running a race with no finish line? Are you growing weary in your efforts, longing for the Lord to return? You may feel like you are all alone. In reality, you are in good company!

King David had a habit of telling God exactly how he was feeling. We have so many psalms and words of encouragement as a result of his honest dialog with the Lord. Consider writing down facts about how you feel when you are engaged in battles. Try articulating the root cause of the conflicts. You could even write out a prayer about the marathon race you feel like you are running.

In the weary times, the real battle is over you. Your defeat is in distraction, busyness, and focus on the things of this world. Fight through the distractions and fix your eyes on Jesus. Direction over time beats perfection for a moment. Return to the intentional pursuit of Jesus.

Intimacy with your Savior during these wearying times will allow you to echo the words of Paul, used in this passage, and loudly exclaim that you have kept the faith! Keep the faith and stay in the fight. Focus on Jesus Christ and keep taking another step in obedience toward Him. Meditate on what God is preparing for you, as you long for His appearing.

Pray this passage back to the Lord, knowing that He will carry you to the finish.

23

Give It Away

**I thank my God always when I remember you in my prayers,
because I hear of your love and of the faith that you have toward
the Lord Jesus and for all the saints, and I pray that the sharing of
your faith may become effective for the full knowledge of every
good thing that is in us for the sake of Christ. For I have derived
much joy and comfort from your love, my brother, because
the hearts of the saints have been refreshed through you.**

PHILEMON 4–7

Do you know someone who would appreciate being refreshed right about now? Someone who could use a pick-me-up in the form of a word of encouragement? Try reading this passage again as if you are reading it to a friend who has been that source of encouragement for you. Maybe they are in need of a word of encouragement, and hearing appreciation from you would be that word.

I have learned that when the Lord brings someone to mind, there is a reason. A call or text message to check in is often met with great appreciation. The same is true when I hear from a faithful friend. Be intentional about refreshing the saints in your life. Consider making a list of people who have refreshed you in the past and a list of people you would like to be there for in the future. By putting others first and refreshing others, we ourselves are refreshed.

Love and faith in Christ always lead to loving others and sharing our faith with them. Reach out to someone and let them know how much they have meant to you in your walk with Christ. Then look for that person God will put in your path. Be prepared to share your faith, your joy, and your love. The hearts of many saints will be refreshed by you.

24

Timely Grace

Since then we have a great high priest who has passed through the heavens, Jesus, the Son of God, let us hold fast our confession. For we do not have a high priest who is unable to sympathize with our weaknesses, but one who in every respect has been tempted as we are, yet without sin. Let us then with confidence draw near to the throne of grace, that we may receive mercy and find grace to help in time of need.

HEBREWS 4:14–16

Jesus knows. Jesus Christ endured all the emotion, physical pain, temptations, and weakness we feel right now. He welcomes our conversation with Him about what we are enduring. And even though He already knows, He will patiently listen and readily sympathize. Jesus felt it all, endured it all, and walked through it all, without sinning.

Consider writing down the weaknesses you are experiencing and offer them in confession and prayer. Add a check mark beside the weaknesses you believe Jesus also endured.

Remember that you were raised with Him and are hidden in Him. Vocalize to the Lord what you are thankful for through Christ. You have nothing to fear. Draw near to the throne of grace with confidence in the One who has already paid the price for your admission. In your time of need, draw near to Jesus.

You are not an outsider begging to be let in—you are a welcome family member. Jesus is the High Priest. He is also now your brother. He knows what you need because He has been there. You will receive mercy. He will provide grace. Believe that you have received it, and go before the Lord today with humble confidence in His ability to show us the mercy we are so desperately in need of at this moment.

25

Strong Encouragement

**So when God desired to show more convincingly to the heirs
of the promise the unchangeable character of his purpose, he
guaranteed it with an oath, so that by two unchangeable things,
in which it is impossible for God to lie, we who have fled for
refuge might have strong encouragement to hold fast to the hope
set before us. We have this as a sure and steadfast anchor of the
soul, a hope that enters into the inner place behind the curtain,
where Jesus has gone as a forerunner on our behalf, having
become a high priest forever after the order of Melchizedek.**

HEBREWS 6:17–20

We marvel at relationships and objects that stand the test of time and tur-moil. We celebrate marriages that last and admire relics uncovered from the depths of the ocean, or from tombs sealed long ago. Nobody would be impressed if archaeologists displayed a mound of sand claiming to have once been something of value. But when they uncover artifacts that have withstood time and the elements, we pay to see them on display.

Every man-made promise is subject to change, and many of them do not hold up very well over time. God seals His promises with an oath. The character of God's purpose has never changed. His promises will continue to hold, because He cannot lie. His oath has endured.

God loves you. Nothing can change this truth. Maybe you need to make a list of failures you think God hasn't considered in His knowledge of you. Are there things you think He doesn't know about or facts you think would cause the Lord to take back His promises?

Consider making a list. Confess the list to the Lord. Then draw a box around your list and an X through the box. You are an heir to the promise that your sins are forgiven through faith in Jesus Christ. Your refuge is now in Christ. Hold fast to this hope! Hope is the sure and steadfast anchor of the soul. Hope keeps us connected in a relationship with Jesus. People, and man-made objects, will let you down at times. God will not.

Is your hope in Jesus? Do you need to transfer your hope in other things so that 100 percent of your hope is in Him?

26

During Testing

Count it all joy, my brothers, when you meet trials of various kinds, for you know that the testing of your faith produces steadfastness. And let steadfastness have its full effect, that you may be perfect and complete, lacking in nothing.

JAMES 1:2–4

If you are like me, you do your best to avoid trials. We look for ways to insulate ourselves and ensure a clear path around various trials. Then, when we fail to avoid trials, we get frustrated. That fog, rock, tree, or unmarked fork in our path is unwelcome and can only serve to hinder us and slow us down for no good reason. We are justified in our joyless annoyance, right?

Scripture gives us a different perspective on trials and even hope in the midst of trials. The trials of life are tests of our faith. Trials of various kinds cause us to move and adjust, endure and reassess. In the midst of trials, faith should prompt us to realign ourselves with the mission and mindset of Christ. Steadfastness and muscle growth is produced in these times.

Are you experiencing trials of various kinds right now? Would making a list of your trials help identify those things and possibly allow for a fresh perspective?

When we joyfully accept God's will in our life, we will gain traction in the direction of Jesus Christ. When we are aligned and gain momentum toward Jesus, He will draw us unto Himself in greater and greater measure, until we are perfect and complete.

The next time you face a trial or don't get your way, consider offering your trial up to the Lord. Can you look at this new trial with a different perspective—one of joy even? Scripture promises positive results when we adopt a godly attitude. Joyfully exclaim your appreciation for the direction toward perfection that will result.

27

He Will Lift You Up

Humble yourselves before the Lord, and he will exalt you.

JAMES 4:10

What a contrast we see when we look at the God of the Bible compared to all other man-made gods. All other gods invite you to come before them, bringing your very best—and if your very best measures up, you get an audience with the god. From Genesis to Revelation, our God consistently encourages us to humbly come before Him—not with hopes that we will measure up based on our gifts or good deeds but with humility. Humility is the result of our preparation to meet with the Lord. The proud heart will skip the preparation and boldly attempt to go before the Lord. God knows your heart.

As we consider who God is and what God has done for us, humility should begin to stir. As we further contemplate who we are and what we have done, humility should displace pride. And when we realize the depth of our sin, in contrast to the all-knowing love of Jesus Christ, humility will allow us a right posture before an Almighty God.

The world is constantly trying to get you to exalt yourself. God promises to exalt you well beyond social media. Being raised with Christ, you will be exalted as Christ is lifted up. The things of this world will have an end. Life with Christ has no end.

Consider writing down ways that you could adopt a humbler attitude. Pray for insight into areas that you have not yet considered.

28

Tested Genuine

May grace and peace be multiplied to you. Blessed be the God and Father of our Lord Jesus Christ! According to his great mercy, he has caused us to be born again to a living hope through the resurrection of Jesus Christ from the dead, to an inheritance that is imperishable, undefiled, and unfading, kept in heaven for you, who by God's power are being guarded through faith for a salvation ready to be revealed in the last time. In this you rejoice, though now for a little while, if necessary, you have been grieved by various trials, so that the tested genuineness of your faith—more precious than gold that perishes though it is tested by fire—may be found to result in praise and glory and honor at the revelation of Jesus Christ.

1 PETER 1:2–7

Are you distracted, even grieved, by various trials occurring in your life right now? I join Peter in praying for grace and peace to be multiplied in you during this trial.

Consider writing down some information about your trial. Where do you believe this trial came from, and what is the impact upon your life? Knowing, and being reminded, that this trial is there to verify the genuineness of your faith in Jesus Christ may be of little consolation right now. However, grace and peace are being offered to you in the midst of your trial. And the right reaction in the midst of trials is to turn to the gift-giver, Jesus. Through faith in Christ, we can praise the God and Father of our Lord Jesus Christ for His great blanket of mercy. His mercy brought you into a living hope that can overshadow your trial.

Add a list of His mercies to what you write down about your trial. The authenticity of your faith is in full bloom when you cry out to the Lord acknowledging your trial and His mercy for you in the fire. Grace and peace have the opportunity to be multiplied in you, and through you, as this trial proves your faith to be genuine. Genuine faith, the gift of God through Jesus Christ, will stand the test of time and trials. Even in this trial, God is guarding you and your faith.

Praise, glory, and honor are His as we, His children, follow Him.

29

He Cares for You

**Humble yourselves, therefore, under the mighty hand of
God so that at the proper time he may exalt you, casting
all your anxieties on him, because he cares for you.**

1 PETER 5:6–7

In our distracted and hurried effort to get to the next thing in our life, we can miss things. In our zeal to complete a passage of Scripture or read through the Bible in a certain time frame, the words might barely penetrate our eyes. Maybe another approach would be helpful. Try committing this passage to memory this week. Meditate on each line and unpack these words of God as you go. Sometimes I start at the end of a passage and work backwards in order to see the words in a new light.

God cares for you. Slow down and appreciate that truth for a day. He not only wants an everlasting relationship with you, He wants to hear about what is bothering you. Consider writing down your list of anxieties under the heading: "God Cares about the Following."

God has wonderfully perfect timing for every occurrence in our lives. He can lift you up—even exalt you—because He is mighty. Of all the biblical figures, God chose the apostle Peter to pen this Word for you. One of the proudest, boldest figures in all of Scripture reminds us that humility comes before exaltation. God chose you, me, and Peter for unique purposes and missions. When we get bogged down by anxiety, we need to remember that God is concerned with everything that concerns us. Humble yourself before the Lord enough to transparently give Him your whole list of anxieties.

30

He Called You

And after you have suffered a little while, the God of all grace, who has called you to his eternal glory in Christ, will himself restore, confirm, strengthen, and establish you. To him be the dominion forever and ever. Amen.

1 PETER 5:10–11

The God you serve has called you to His eternal glory in Jesus Christ. Think back to when this truth first held your fascination and wonder. Consider writing down the first time, or the last time, the truth of God's calling felt personal to you. Your gaze was up, the smile came easily, and His praise flowed from you. The truth of God's calling for you is still constant and unchangeable.

What may have changed are your circumstances. Hardships, disappointments, trials, and suffering can cause us to lower our gaze and fix our eyes on ourselves or our circumstances. You are in good company if you are suffering. The God of all grace wants to hear from you in the midst of your suffering. His Word clearly and consistently reminds us that He uses trials for our good and for His glory.

The God of all grace loves you and still calls you to His eternal glory. He Himself will restore, confirm, strengthen, and establish you.

To God be the glory forever and ever.

31

Granted to Us

**His divine power has granted to us all things that pertain to life
and godliness, through the knowledge of him who called us to
his own glory and excellence, by which he has granted to us his
precious and very great promises, so that through them you may
become partakers of the divine nature, having escaped from
the corruption that is in the world because of sinful desire.**

2 PETER 1:3–4

Sinful desires hamper us and pull us down to the world's level. We each have our own mix of sinful desires, but in reality, they all look the same to the Lord. Consider writing a list of the sinful desires that come to your mind. Remember that Jesus breaks the cords that would tie us to this world. Through His divine power, we are given everything we need for life and godliness.

He called you to know Him personally. You are miraculously allowed to partake in His divine nature and be cloaked in His glory and excellence. Change your focus from the things of this world to His precious and great promises.

The desires that would hold you and keep you like gravity will give way to Jesus. Focus on Him and His promises.

32

You May Know

**I write these things to you who believe in the name of the
Son of God, that you may know that you have eternal life.**

1 JOHN 5:13

Do you believe in the name of the Son of God? Jesus of Nazareth claimed to be the one and only Son of God. Scripture says He lived a sinless life, loved without boundaries or borders, challenged our entire worldview, and rose from the dead after being executed in a most heinous manner. Believing in this Jesus always results in action by the believer.

God wants you to know that you will have an eternal life with Him in Heaven. The gift is ours to appreciate now, even though it will be realized in the future. Distractions and worldly affairs will drown out the song of our Savior if we allow it. If you question your salvation or lack confidence in what Christ did for you, take those concerns to the Lord in prayer. You can know, today, that you are His forever.

Consider a written thank-you note to the Lord for His promises. Maybe focusing on and appreciating the promise of eternal life will help put our worldly affairs in proper perspective.

33

He Is Able

**Now to him who is able to keep you from stumbling
and to present you blameless before the presence of his
glory with great joy, to the only God, our Savior, through
Jesus Christ our Lord, be glory, majesty, dominion, and
authority, before all time and now and forever. Amen.**

JUDE 24–25

Forever, beginning before the advent of time, through this day and beyond, God is praised. His glory, majesty, dominion, and authority have no end. We have but to join the chorus of His praise. Are you actively participating in the chorus?

In the midst of the praises, our Savior sees where you are walking and knows exactly how each step and each breath feels. He understands your pain, longings, anxiety, and fears. He cares enough to offer to keep you from stumbling. He is able to keep you from stumbling even when you think a stumble is inevitable. He has promised to take you into His glory and present you as blameless. And He will gladly do this "with great joy."

You are going to be presented before the presence of His glory, joyfully. You are not sliding into Heaven by some slim margin. Your entry will be met with great joy, through Jesus Christ our Lord, and for His glory.

Consider writing down accolades you would ascribe to your Savior. Do you need to add any words of thanksgiving to your list?

Praise God through Jesus Christ, our Lord—even now, especially now.

34

My Savior

**Make me to know your ways, O Lord; teach me your
paths. Lead me in your truth and teach me, for you are the
God of my salvation; for you I wait all the day long.**

PSALM 25:4–5

Can we join David in claiming this passage? Yes, we can!

The first part is the humble request for revelation. The ask is in three parts:

1. Show me your ways.
2. Teach me your path.
3. Lead me in your truth.

When we humble ourselves to the point of coachability and teachability, the Lord will open the floodgates of understanding.

The second part is the great acknowledgment: For you are God my Savior! This is an alignment of God as the possessor and grantor of the gift of salvation and us as the undeserving recipients.

The final part is hard for me: After asking for His teaching and acknowledging His status as Savior, do we then trust Him with our daily lives? We trust and acknowledge on Christmas and Easter. Maybe we are faithful to be open to His leading on most Sunday mornings. Some of us feel good about Sundays, and daily as we pray before going to work, and again falling into bed. David says his hope was in the Lord all day long. I would like to get to the point in my relationship where I can say that too, with complete integrity.

God made you in His image, then sacrificed His Son to allow for a never-ending relationship wherein He would pour every good gift imaginable. Ask Him for these wonderful gifts, acknowledging Him as your Savior. Lean into Him in every part of your day today.

When we find that we are not leaned into Him, not trusting in Him for outcomes, or unsatisfied with His provision, maybe we fall back on this passage and ask for a new start?

In our "do-over," we can humbly ask God to take the lead and show us the way. He can teach us His ways when we are submitted and listening. He will lead, patiently teach, and lovingly show you the best course for you to follow. He is the God of your salvation, and He is worth the wait.

35

Help Comes

**I lift up my eyes to the hills. From where does my help come?
My help comes from the Lord, who made heaven and earth.
He will not let your foot be moved; he who keeps you will not
slumber. Behold, he who keeps Israel will neither slumber
nor sleep. The Lord is your keeper; the Lord is your shade
on your right hand. The sun shall not strike you by day, nor
the moon by night. The Lord will keep you from all evil; he
will keep your life. The Lord will keep your going out and
your coming in from this time forth and forevermore.**

PSALM 121

We often see this verse on a painting depicting mountains or tree-covered hills. I appreciate the mountain scenes, but that is not from where our help comes. Our help comes from the Lord. He is your keeper, and He does not rest from loving you.

Could you use some help right now? Are you at the end of your rope, having exhausted all your knowledge and efforts? And now you look to see that the problems, issues, and situation still exist? Maybe it is time to look up. Lift your eyes off the problem and look to the solution.

The Lord reminds us, through the psalmist, that He is a vigilant God. He is vigilant about your care and well-being. We are, at times, tempted to think the Lord is far off or inattentive to our lives. We are strongly reminded that He cares about the very same details concerning you.

Maybe you need a reminder of who is actually going to answer your cry for help? Consider combing this passage and writing down who your help is and what He is prepared to do for you. Your help does not come from the hills. Your help created the hills. He does not take breaks from loving you or caring for you.

Look to the Lord.

36

Worth the Wait

**Out of the depths I cry to you, O Lord! O Lord, hear my voice!
Let your ears be attentive to the voice of my pleas for mercy! If
you, O Lord, should mark iniquities, O Lord, who could stand?
But with you there is forgiveness, that you may be feared. I wait
for the Lord, my soul waits, and in his word I hope; my soul
waits for the Lord more than watchmen for the morning, more
than watchmen for the morning. O Israel, hope in the Lord! For
with the Lord there is steadfast love, and with him is plentiful
redemption. And he will redeem Israel from all his iniquities.**

PSALM 130

The psalmist reassures us that the Lord has an abundance of mercy, for-giveness, love, and redemption. Are you ready for a cup full of these from the Lord? I think we would all say yes to a package of mercy, forgiveness, and love, wrapped with the bow of redemption. Maybe you can freely acknowledge these gifts from the Lord, but right now you just don't feel them. Emotions are important and not to be discounted. However, the psalmist is here describing, in my opinion, that place of hopeful waiting, not the place of good feelings. Have our feelings grown similarly cold to the destructive consequences of our sin?

The psalmist cries out to the Lord and immediately acknowledges his iniquities. He is in the depths and crying for help against the consequences of his iniquities. When was the last time you truly confessed sin? Would it help to make a list and pray that list to the God who offers the forgiveness, mercy, and love?

The psalmist does not cry, plead for mercy, then set out to fix his own problems. He aligns himself rightly with a Holy God and then waits for God. His waiting is more patient than a vigilant soldier who stays the night hoping for the morning. We wait for the Lord at a soul level as we embrace His love, mercy, forgiveness, and redemption.

37

God Answers

May the Lord answer you in the day of trouble! May the name
of the God of Jacob protect you! May he send you help from the
sanctuary and give you support from Zion! May he remember all
your offerings and regard with favor your burnt sacrifices! Selah
May he grant you your heart's desire and fulfill all your plans! May
we shout for joy over your salvation, and in the name of our God
set up our banners! May the Lord fulfill all your petitions! Now I
know that the Lord saves his anointed; he will answer him from
his holy heaven with the saving might of his right hand. Some
trust in chariots and some in horses, but we trust in the name of
the Lord our God. They collapse and fall, but we rise and stand
upright. O Lord, save the king! May he answer us when we call.

PSALM 20

This is a powerful psalm of support. My mom "gave" me this psalm as a word of encouragement during a time of wonder and wander in my life. Years later, I began to memorize Psalm 20, recognizing the power of God's Word for all situations. This is a wonderful psalm to proclaim back to the Lord in worship and prayer.

How awesome that God would care enough to see that this word of encouragement would make its way to you when you need support. There are so many future acts that we can look to, and be hopeful for, from the Lord. The variable seems to be in where we (people) place our trust. Those who trust in the world (horses and chariots—bank accounts and other people) are destined to fall. But those who trust in the Lord will rise and stand firm. The Lord saves His anointed!

Is your trust evenly spread across multiple options like a diversified investment portfolio? Do you trust in your own strength, the power of contacts in your life, your savings, or good luck? Or is your trust only in the name of the Lord your God?

May He grant you your heart's desires and fulfill all your plans as you trust in Him.

38

His Name Is Majestic

O Lord, our Lord, how majestic is your name in all the earth! You have set your glory above the heavens. Out of the mouth of babies and infants, you have established strength because of your foes, to still the enemy and the avenger. When I look at your heavens, the work of your fingers, the moon and the stars, which you have set in place, what is man that you are mindful of him, and the son of man that you care for him? Yet you have made him a little lower than the heavenly beings and crowned him with glory and honor. You have given him dominion over the works of your hands; you have put all things under his feet, all sheep and oxen, and also the beasts of the field, the birds of the heavens, and the fish of the sea, whatever passes along the paths of the seas. O Lord, our Lord, how majestic is your name in all the earth!

PSALM 8

Sometimes we need to pause our own motion and realign ourselves with God Almighty. When was the last time you got alone with your God and just sang a line from a hymn to Him? The first sentence of this psalm will forever be set in my mind to a melody I learned in junior high school church choir. Try singing this sentence to the Lord making up the notes on your own. Thirteen words set to your own tune, just between you and the Lord.

Consider making your goal, sometime during this week, to dissect this psalm. Dig into this passage and see if the Lord speaks to you in the process. Ten minutes of effort. Can we pause our work, still our agenda, and set aside ten minutes to meditate on God's Word?

As part of your meditation, consider writing down all the points of majesty listed for God in the passage above. How majestic is the name of the Lord your God? Try reading this psalm out loud. See if praising God with His own Word doesn't help to right-size your ambitions, cares, and concerns.

He is mindful of you. He had you in mind during the planning phase of creation, and He loves hearing from you. Praise His name first, then tell Him your plans.

39

Safe House

How lovely is your dwelling place, O Lord of hosts! My soul longs, yes, faints for the courts of the Lord; my heart and flesh sing for joy to the living God. Even the sparrow finds a home, and the swallow a nest for herself, where she may lay her young, at your altars, O Lord of hosts, my King and my God. Blessed are those who dwell in your house, ever singing your praise! Selah Blessed are those whose strength is in you, in whose heart are the highways to Zion. As they go through the Valley of Baca they make it a place of springs; the early rain also covers it with pools. They go from strength to strength; each one appears before God in Zion. O Lord God of hosts, hear my prayer; give ear, O God of Jacob! Selah Behold our shield, O God; look on the face of your anointed! For a day in your courts is better than a thousand elsewhere. I would rather be a doorkeeper in the house of my God than dwell in the tents of wickedness. For the Lord God is a sun and shield; the Lord bestows favor and honor. No good thing does he withhold from those who walk uprightly. O Lord of hosts, blessed is the one who trusts in you!

PSALM 84

Every fiber of the psalmist is in joyful praise of the Lord. He is camped out in a relationship with God, constantly pursuing Him and spending time with Him. His heart and his flesh are bursting with joy toward the Lord. The psalmist rightly identifies that his strength is in the Lord, and he is ever singing the Lord's praise.

Even the psalmist, however, goes through the Valley of Baca (weeping) with flowing grief. And yet, he is still considered strong. This is not a portrait of someone who does not feel the need to cry out to the Lord—he is begging the Lord to hear him and look upon him. Can you identify with the desire to be looked upon favorably by God? Would you like to identify more closely with Psalm 84?

I see four attributes in this psalm that garner the Lord's blessings. Can you identify them in the passage, and in your life? Lean into the Lord and sing His praise—especially when you are in the Valley of Baca. He is your sun and shield, bestowing favor and honor.

Consider highlighting the parts of this passage that resonate with you. Underline those expectations you have as you continue to seek your King and your God.

40

Joyful Noise

**Make a joyful noise to the Lord, all the earth! Serve the Lord
with gladness! Come into his presence with singing! Know that
the Lord, he is God! It is he who made us, and we are his; we
are his people, and the sheep of his pasture. Enter his gates
with thanksgiving, and his courts with praise! Give thanks to
him; bless his name! For the Lord is good; his steadfast love
endures forever, and his faithfulness to all generations.**

PSALM 100

What would it take for you to embrace Psalm 100, right now, and make a joyful noise to the Lord? Maybe your head is full of concerns and issues that would like to keep you from singing. Maybe your heart is heavy with the weight of the world. Or maybe you are on a crowded airplane where you are self-conscious of your presence among others.

Pause the distractions for just a minute and be reminded that the Lord is God. He made you. You belong to Him. The Lord is good and faithful, with an everlasting love for you.

Maybe today your joyful noise for Almighty God is just to read Psalm 100 out loud. Maybe tomorrow it sounds like clapping when you read the psalm again. Try smiling as you give thanks to the Lord for the great things He has done.

Find one way to serve the Lord this week and do it with intentional gladness. The Lord knows your heart. He will accept all kinds of joyful noise from you.

41

This Is the Day!

This is the day that the Lord has made; let us rejoice and be glad in it. Save us, we pray, O Lord! O Lord, we pray, give us success! Blessed is he who comes in the name of the Lord! We bless you from the house of the Lord. The Lord is God, and he has made his light to shine upon us. Bind the festal sacrifice with cords, up to the horns of the altar! You are my God, and I will give thanks to you; you are my God; I will extol you. Oh give thanks to the Lord, for he is good; for his steadfast love endures forever!

PSALM 118:24–29

This passage is a call for intentionality for good reason—because the Lord is God! God gave us this day, and at this day's end, if we have accomplished nothing else, let us have rejoiced and been glad in it.

As we align ourselves with our God, we cannot help but acknowledge the One who has made His light to shine upon us. We give the sacrifice of our thanksgiving, joyfully, with gladness. God doesn't need possessions made from earthly materials, like gold or money. He wants the sacrifice of our hearts yielded to Him. This doesn't happen in a drive-by meeting with God. This is the intentional pause of all other competing idols in our life and a recognition of the Lord God. He is Creator God, Savior God, steadfast and loving. He is blessing and provider God. This is the God who made this day and wants to see his children rejoice. Enjoy his good and perfect gift.

Save us, O Lord, and give us success as we follow You.
You are my God, and I will give thanks to You.

42

God Will Provide

**After these things God tested Abraham and said to him,
"Abraham!" And he said, "Here I am." He said, "Take your son,
your only son Isaac, whom you love, and go to the land of Moriah,
and offer him there as a burnt offering on one of the mountains
of which I shall tell you." So Abraham rose early in the morning,
saddled his donkey, and took two of his young men with him,
and his son Isaac. And he cut the wood for the burnt offering and
arose and went to the place of which God had told him. On the
third day Abraham lifted up his eyes and saw the place from afar.
Then Abraham said to his young men, "Stay here with the donkey;
I and the boy will go over there and worship and come again to
you." And Abraham took the wood of the burnt offering and laid
it on Isaac his son. And he took in his hand the fire and the knife.
So they went both of them together. And Isaac said to his father
Abraham, "My father!" And he said, "Here I am, my son." He said,
"Behold, the fire and the wood, but where is the lamb for a burnt
offering?" Abraham said, "God will provide for himself the lamb
for a burnt offering, my son." So they went both of them together.**

GENESIS 22:1–8

Abraham absolutely loved his son Isaac. If you recall, there was quite a
story to the long-awaited birth of this child. Isaac was God's promise to
Abraham. And yet, the Lord asked Abraham to turn around and sacrifice
(kill) his son as an offering to the Lord. Has God asked you to make sacrifices? Do you wonder how a loving God could make promises while He
asks you to do things in contrast to those promises?

God was testing Abraham. God's plan, unbeknownst to Abraham, was
to wait and see Abraham's faithfulness in action. At the last second, with
Isaac bound on the altar, God intervened and told Abraham to spare Isaac.
Do you think God loves you any less than He loved Abraham?

You, too, will be tested. Make a plan to be found faithful. God's testing
will prove your faith to be genuine, and you will learn more about the Lord
in the process. Lean in and listen for the call—then respond with, "Here I
am!" as you follow His voice.

43

Stillness

When Pharaoh drew near, the people of Israel lifted up their eyes, and behold, the Egyptians were marching after them, and they feared greatly. And the people of Israel cried out to the Lord. They said to Moses, "Is it because there are no graves in Egypt that you have taken us away to die in the wilderness? What have you done to us in bringing us out of Egypt? Is not this what we said to you in Egypt: 'Leave us alone that we may serve the Egyptians'? For it would have been better for us to serve the Egyptians than to die in the wilderness." And Moses said to the people, "Fear not, stand firm, and see the salvation of the Lord, which he will work for you today. For the Egyptians whom you see today, you shall never see again. The Lord will fight for you, and you have only to be silent."

EXODUS 14:10–14

God has a plan for you, just as He did for the enslaved Israelites. The Israelites were allowed to witness the miracles God did through Moses and experience the first Passover. If that wasn't enough, He parted the waters of the Red Sea and gave them a path to freedom.

Has God provided mightily in your life? Consider writing down some of His faithful provisions for you.

After all these generous acts, the Israelites began to sarcastically grumble. After all they had witnessed and experienced, they still had fear. Can you relate?

The Israelites were afraid of what they saw—their captors gaining ground on the freshly released, former slaves. Fear gripped them, and they were ready to give up—wishing they had never left the captivity of the Egyptians.

Have you followed the sound of the Lord's voice and now wonder what you were thinking? Giving in to fear will not help. Moses wasn't perfect either, but he was convinced the Lord would fight on their behalf. Stand firm, like Moses, and look for the salvation of the Lord instead. God has a plan for you, just like He did for Moses and the Israelites.

44

Take Courage

"Be strong and courageous, for you shall cause this people to inherit the land that I swore to their fathers to give them. Only be strong and very courageous, being careful to do according to all the law that Moses my servant commanded you. Do not turn from it to the right hand or to the left, that you may have good success wherever you go. This Book of the Law shall not depart from your mouth, but you shall meditate on it day and night, so that you may be careful to do according to all that is written in it. For then you will make your way prosperous, and then you will have good success. Have I not commanded you? Be strong and courageous. Do not be frightened, and do not be dismayed, for the Lord your God is with you wherever you go."

JOSHUA 1:6–9

How might God be asking you, like Joshua, to be strong and courageous? God was specific in His instruction to Joshua, that being obedient was paramount. We tend to think of obedience in connection with the big things of life. I believe it takes strength and courage to be obedient to God in the little things, even the unseen things.

The Lord's ultimate desire is an everlasting relationship with you. You can pursue a relationship with Him through meditating on His Word and speaking the truth. Your pursuit of Him may be the example that draws another person to a relationship with Him. Joshua needed to get his act together because God was about to use Him to lead His people into the Promised Land.

Your obedience—your strength and courage—will be used by the Lord in ways you cannot imagine. We don't have to have all the answers in order to obey the command to be strong and courageous in our faith. Seek Him. The Lord, your God, is with you.

45

Finding Favor

As she continued praying before the Lord, Eli observed her mouth. Hannah was speaking in her heart; only her lips moved, and her voice was not heard. Therefore Eli took her to be a drunken woman. And Eli said to her, "How long will you go on being drunk? Put your wine away from you." But Hannah answered, "No, my lord, I am a woman troubled in spirit. I have drunk neither wine nor strong drink, but I have been pouring out my soul before the Lord. Do not regard your servant as a worthless woman, for all along I have been speaking out of my great anxiety and vexation." Then Eli answered, "Go in peace, and the God of Israel grant your petition that you have made to him." And she said, "Let your servant find favor in your eyes." Then the woman went her way and ate, and her face was no longer sad.

1 SAMUEL 1:12–18

Eli encountered a woman whose face detailed the anxiety and vexation she was enduring in her heart. She was troubled in spirit and had come to the temple to pray before the Lord. She even told Eli that she was pouring out her soul before the Lord.

There is no magic verse for getting the peace of the Lord. There is no set of steps that guarantee a desired response to your petition. Continue praying before the Lord like Hannah, speaking to Him from your heart, pouring out your soul before Him.

Consider writing down those things that are vexing you and causing anxiety. Pray over your list and offer these things up to the Lord. Then go in peace. The Lord hears you and knows how to provide for His children. Hannah had likely fasted over her prayers. Has your anxiety caused you to fast from something you enjoy? Give thanksgiving to God over a meal or fun activity.

I pray that God will grant your petition and turn your anxiety into peace.

46

Good to Be Generous

And David said, "Is there still anyone left of the house of Saul, that I may show him kindness for Jonathan's sake?" Now there was a servant of the house of Saul whose name was Ziba, and they called him to David. And the king said to him, "Are you Ziba?" And he said, "I am your servant." And the king said, "Is there not still someone of the house of Saul, that I may show the kindness of God to him?" Ziba said to the king, "There is still a son of Jonathan; he is crippled in his feet." The king said to him, "Where is he?" And Ziba said to the king, "He is in the house of Machir the son of Ammiel, at Lo-debar." Then King David sent and brought him from the house of Machir the son of Ammiel, at Lo-debar. And Mephibosheth the son of Jonathan, son of Saul, came to David and fell on his face and paid homage. And David said, "Mephibosheth!" And he answered, "Behold, I am your servant." And David said to him, "Do not fear, for I will show you kindness for the sake of your father Jonathan, and I will restore to you all the land of Saul your father, and you shall eat at my table always." And he paid homage and said, "What is your servant, that you should show regard for a dead dog such as I?"

2 SAMUEL 9:1–8

Are you on the lookout for someone to whom you can show the kindness of God? The newly crowned King David went out of his way to look for anyone he could bless from the house of Saul. David's pursuit of kindness came after the deposed (now dead) king attempted to kill David. They discovered Mephibosheth, crippled and hiding, fearing for his life, in Lo-debar.

Mephibosheth must have thought he was being taken back to Jerusalem for public execution. That would have made sense at that time and place in history. Instead, David gives him an enormous portion of the kingdom and a permanent seat at the king's family table.

Be open to the possibility and opportunity to bless someone in your life who thinks of themselves as a dead dog, like Mephibosheth. It seems that David delighted in showing this unexpected kindness. Maybe blessing someone else will create delight within you as well.

47

Wisdom Supreme

"And now, O Lord my God, you have made your servant king in place of David my father, although I am but a little child. I do not know how to go out or come in. And your servant is in the midst of your people whom you have chosen, a great people, too many to be numbered or counted for multitude. Give your servant therefore an understanding mind to govern your people, that I may discern between good and evil, for who is able to govern this your great people?" It pleased the Lord that Solomon had asked this. And God said to him, "Because you have asked this, and have not asked for yourself long life or riches or the life of your enemies, but have asked for yourself understanding to discern what is right, behold, I now do according to your word."

1 KINGS 3:7–12

At this juncture in his life, Solomon has rightly yielded before the Lord. He has been made the King of Israel, and yet he is willing to acknowledge the Lord as *his* King. Solomon goes further in describing himself as a servant and a little child.

Do we have the order right in our hearts? Is God number one? Solomon lifts up the people of Israel as number two and identifies himself as a servant in their midst. He humbles himself, claiming no knowledge or understanding to do even the simplest tasks. In his humility, he has the right attitude and alignment.

Do we have the right attitude and alignment? God knew Solomon's heart when he asked for understanding. God knows your heart as well. The next step may be to ask for a humble attitude and a right alignment with your God and King.

48

Perfect Placement

**And they told Mordecai what Esther had said. Then Mordecai
told them to reply to Esther, "Do not think to yourself that in
the king's palace you will escape any more than all the other
Jews. For if you keep silent at this time, relief and deliverance
will rise for the Jews from another place, but you and your
father's house will perish. And who knows whether you
have not come to the kingdom for such a time as this?"**

ESTHER 4:12–14

Mordecai has a penetrating faith and a deep trust in God. In his strength, he gave great advice and encouragement to Esther. His faith, however, was not dependent upon the outcome of his advice to Esther. Rather, his faith was rightly placed in the Lord.

Mordecai firmly believed that relief and deliverance for the Jews was coming. He challenged Esther to consider that the time had come, through her position as queen. Even if Esther continued in her fear, or failed in her attempts, Mordecai was confident in God, not people.

Are you waiting on relief and deliverance in one or more areas of your life? Consider writing down those things you are hoping to see. Maybe those should be lifted up to God as a prayer request? Consider, too, like Esther, that you may have a role in God's plan for the relief you are hoping to see. You may be in the perfect spot for such a time as this.

49

Blessing in the Pit

**Then Job arose and tore his robe and shaved his head and fell
on the ground and worshiped. And he said, "Naked I came
from my mother's womb, and naked shall I return. The Lord
gave, and the Lord has taken away; blessed be the name of the
Lord." In all this Job did not sin or charge God with wrong.**

JOB 1:20–22

At the end of the book of Job, we learn that God blessed the latter part of Job's life even more than the first. At the beginning of the book of Job, we see that Job is living a blessed life. Everything in Job's life was worthy of a Facebook post. Family, possessions, prestige—Job was living a big life.

When all that changed, Job made a decision. He humbled himself and went before a Holy God. Outwardly, Job tore his clothes and shaved his head—both signs of distress and humility. Then he centered himself on the Lord by uttering truth. In the midst of his pain, frustration, and humility, Job praises God.

Is this how we handle stress and distress? Consider writing down those circumstances causing distress in your life. Then follow Job in a pattern of humility, truth, and praise. Sometimes we need an example to follow. The Lord gave us the story of Job and his faithfulness in the pit to encourage and teach us. When we are in the process of the Lord's giving, we tend to think of it as a blessing. When we are in the opposite process of the potentially painful removing of something in our life by the Lord, we can tend to see it as a curse. Our example is Job. He chose to grieve the loss and still praise the name of the Lord.

50

Appreciating God

**What gain has the worker from his toil? I have seen the business
that God has given to the children of man to be busy with. He has
made everything beautiful in its time. Also, he has put eternity
into man's heart, yet so that he cannot find out what God has done
from the beginning to the end. I perceived that there is nothing
better for them than to be joyful and to do good as long as they
live; also that everyone should eat and drink and take pleasure in
all his toil—this is God's gift to man. I perceived that whatever God
does endures forever; nothing can be added to it, nor anything
taken from it. God has done it, so that people fear before him.**

ECCLESIASTES 3:9–14

God is the ultimate giver of good gifts. God is wise and exacting in His
benevolence toward the goal of us having a right understanding of Him.
You were created for a purpose. Unique in all creation, you have a job to
do and a God who wants to see us busy, and joyful, in our work (just like
He is). There is a beautiful mystery in His purposes, and we are allowed
glimpses when we joyfully lean into Him. This message is consistent from
the Old Testament to the New.

How many gifts from God do you see in this passage? One of the
greatest gifts is God's hope that we would take pleasure in this life. You
were made to enjoy Him forever! His ultimate gift was Jesus, who said He
"came that we may have life and have it to the fullest" (John 10:10). Are you
enjoying the pleasure of this life to the fullest?

Pursue the Lord in and through your good work. Give Him back the
gift of a joyful heart. Consider writing down those things for which you
would like to thank Him this week.

51

Gracious Guidance

Therefore the Lord waits to be gracious to you, and therefore he exalts himself to show mercy to you. For the Lord is a God of justice; blessed are all those who wait for him. For a people shall dwell in Zion, in Jerusalem; you shall weep no more. He will surely be gracious to you at the sound of your cry. As soon as he hears it, he answers you. And though the Lord give you the bread of adversity and the water of affliction, yet your Teacher will not hide himself anymore, but your eyes shall see your Teacher. And your ears shall hear a word behind you, saying, "This is the way, walk in it," when you turn to the right or when you turn to the left.

ISAIAH 30:18–21

In this passage, the Lord is specifically identified as the Teacher. The lessons may be hard, but your Teacher is committed to you. You will know and appreciate more if you humble yourself and wait for your Teacher to show you the way. The Lord is, and is going to be, gracious to you. You need to know and appreciate this truth, especially if you are walking in adversity and affliction right now. You may be tempted to fix your own circumstances, or pray this meal (the bread of adversity and the water of affliction) away from yourself.

The Lord hears the sound of your cry for help. He will help you discern the next, best steps. As you relate with Him, check to be sure you understand. You will be assured that you are right where He wants you. God has a perfect will for you. God is also perfect in timing. His timing is not always aligned with our timing, which means our will has to submit to His will. God's will is also perfect in justice, graciousness, and mercy. The Teacher knows you and knows how best to bless and provide for you. Sometimes that means affliction, adversity, and waiting.

Trust in the gracious perfection of God and His loving will for your life. Wait for the Lord and let Him teach you. Humbled and submitted, with perfect timing, you will hear the voice of the Lord.

52

Walk, Run, Fly

Have you not known? Have you not heard? The Lord is the everlasting God, the Creator of the ends of the earth. He does not faint or grow weary; his understanding is unsearchable. He gives power to the faint, and to him who has no might he increases strength. Even youths shall faint and be weary, and young men shall fall exhausted; but they who wait for the Lord shall renew their strength; they shall mount up with wings like eagles; they shall run and not be weary; they shall walk and not faint.

ISAIAH 40:28–31

We can be tempted to read this passage and hastily conclude that running without growing weary and soaring like an eagle will come from having read these words during our time of need. Scripture, however, does not convey that message.

This passage first reminds us of an aligning truth about the nature of our God: He is the everlasting Creator God, with unlimited power and wisdom. This is the God who loves you, cares about you, and is prepared to provide for you. He has resources stored up for you. And they will likely remain stored up while we struggle in our own power to fix and control our situation.

As we are advised in so many other passages, we are told here to wait. When we anticipate God's timing and do things of our own accord, the power is absent. When we succeed under our own power, we take glory away from the Lord. We may be tempted, like a young person, to trust in our own strength and our own wisdom. But those who wait for the Lord will find His resources at their disposal. Only then will we know the true joy of mounting up with wings like eagles. Only when we have waited and are swept up in the power and will of God do we walk and not grow faint.

Check to see that your will is submitted to the Lord. Wait on the everlasting God, the Creator of the universe.

High-Octane Challenge

1. Sin in the Camp—Joshua 7:10–13
2. Choose Now—Joshua 24:14–15
3. What Do You Brag About?—Jeremiah 9:23–26
4. Armed and Ready—Matthew 4:1–11
5. Blessed Outcomes—Matthew 5:1–12
6. Deeper Impact—Matthew 5:27–30
7. Goal Setting—Matthew 5:43–48
8. Your Will Be Done—Matthew 6:5–13
9. I Know You—Matthew 7:21–23
10. Hearing vs. Doing—Matthew 7:24–27
11. Beware—Matthew 10:16–22
12. Loss of Life—Matthew 10:37–39
13. From the Heart—Matthew 18:21–35
14. Love—Matthew 22:34–40
15. Inside Out—Matthew 23:23–26
16. Why the Hard Heart?—Mark 6:45–52
17. Defiled Inside—Mark 7:14–23
18. Your Attention Please—Luke 5:1–11
19. The Word of God—John 1:1–13
20. Love One Another—John 13:34
21. Keep It Simple—John 14:15
22. Plugged In—John 15:1–8
23. Restoration—John 21:15–19
24. Uncommon Boldness—Acts 4:8–13
25. Obey God or Man?—Acts 5:27–32
26. Actual Truth—Proverbs 24:12

Have I not commanded you? Be strong and courageous.
Do not be frightened, and do not be dismayed, for
the Lord your God is with you wherever you go.

JOSHUA 1:9

1

Sin in the Camp

The Lord said to Joshua, "Get up! Why have you fallen on your face? Israel has sinned; they have transgressed my covenant that I commanded them; they have taken some of the devoted things; they have stolen and lied and put them among their own belongings. Therefore the people of Israel cannot stand before their enemies. They turn their backs before their enemies, because they have become devoted for destruction. I will be with you no more, unless you destroy the devoted things from among you. Get up! Consecrate the people and say, 'Consecrate yourselves for tomorrow; for thus says the Lord, God of Israel, "There are devoted things in your midst, O Israel. You cannot stand before your enemies until you take away the devoted things from among you."

JOSHUA 7:10–13

Joshua did not know about Achan stealing articles from the plunder of Jericho. The next battle after Jericho was the battle of Ai. The Israelites were routed, and Joshua was confused, even frustrated. In his confusion and frustration, Joshua turned to the Lord. Achan's sin impacted the whole of Israel and would have to be dealt with before the favor of the Lord could return.

Is there sin in your camp? Are you ignoring disobedience in your own life, hoping it will just go away without consequence? Are you, at the same time, frustrated at current and ongoing circumstances that are not resolving in your favor? Is there sin in your camp?

Sin in your camp is no less tolerable by the Lord now than it was during the time of Joshua. The plunder under our house may be in the form of a different hidden sin, but we should not expect a better outcome. Like Joshua, go before the Lord and ask for revelation. Consider making some notes about what God reveals to you as you pray through a transparent review of your daily activity, dealings, web browsing, and thought life.

Identify the sin in your camp and take it before the Lord. We have forgiveness through the death and resurrection of Jesus Christ. We cannot expect the blessing of the Lord when we have unreconciled sin in our camp.

2

Choose Now

"Now therefore fear the Lord and serve him in sincerity and
in faithfulness. Put away the gods that your fathers served
beyond the River and in Egypt, and serve the Lord. And if it is
evil in your eyes to serve the Lord, choose this day whom you
will serve, whether the gods your fathers served in the region
beyond the River, or the gods of the Amorites in whose land you
dwell. But as for me and my house, we will serve the Lord."

JOSHUA 24:14–15

How many times have we called upon this verse, claimed this verse, and championed ourselves in the name of Joshua 24:15? If you are like me, you have an artistic rendering of this verse hanging somewhere in your home or office as a reminder of whom we choose to serve.

What does serving the Lord mean to you? Is this more of a biblically patriotic notion, or is it acknowledging your actual willingness to forsake everything in the service of our God? When you pledge yourself and your household, what does that include? Does it include the house, the cars too, the 401(k), and every other form of worldly security? Is there anything you are not willing to give up?

The Bible says to "fear" the Lord (consistently from Old to New Testament, such as in 1 Peter 2:17 and this passage). I don't think this means to live in fear so much as it means to have proper respect and humility in acknowledging who He really is: God Almighty. We are further advised (above) to "serve Him with sincerity and in faithfulness." I suspect we can all rally behind the proud declaration, "But as for me and my house," however, the test is in our follow-through. Real life will provide many opportunities for us to prove our faith genuine and make good on the pledge of our service to the Lord.

Consider making some notes about what this means right now in your walk with the Lord. What would you like this to look like one year from now?

3

What Do You Brag About?

JEREMIAH 9:23–26

God is not a fan of falsehood. If our love for Him has remained in the shallowness of those things we effortlessly do for visual approval, then we have checked some dutiful boxes, but missed the relationship. The Israelites must have been taken aback when Jeremiah presented this challenge. I bet the shout down was on, as he accused them of being uncircumcised and maybe didn't even hear *in heart*. Of course the Israelites were circumcised! They, like us, can claim all manner of righteousness in dutifully checking the required boxes. And the response from the Lord, in both the Old and New Testament (Matthew 7) is the same: Do you know me?

All the gifts listed in this passage are from the Lord: wisdom, might, and riches. Praise God from whom every blessing flows! Hopefully you recognize that those are gifts given to us, like talents, to be used for His glory. And if you need to brag or boast, let's hear about how great your understanding of the Lord is, or how great your relationship with Him is right now.

God delights in loving you. He is passionate about justice and righteousness on earth. He gave you gifts, that you might delight yourself in pursuing His will on earth. Are you using your gifts for love, justice, and righteousness? Just like in the parable of the talents (Matthew 25), you will be asked to give an account of how you used your riches, wisdom, and might. How is that conversation going to go?

Consider making some notes about some of the gifts you are thankful for and how you have used them for His kingdom.

4

Armed and Ready

**Then Jesus was led up by the Spirit into the wilderness to be tempted by the
devil. And after fasting forty days and forty nights, he was hungry. And the
tempter came and said to him, "If you are the Son of God, command these
stones to become loaves of bread." But he answered, "It is written, 'Man shall
not live by bread alone, but by every word that comes from the mouth of God.'"
Then the devil took him to the holy city and set him on the pinnacle of the
temple and said to him, "If you are the Son of God, throw yourself down, for it is
written, 'He will command his angels concerning you,' and 'On their hands they
will bear you up, lest you strike your foot against a stone.'" Jesus said to him,
"Again it is written, 'You shall not put the Lord your God to the test.'" Again,
the devil took him to a very high mountain and showed him all the kingdoms
of the world and their glory. And he said to him, "All these I will give you, if you
will fall down and worship me." Then Jesus said to him, "Be gone, Satan! For it
is written, 'You shall worship the Lord your God and him only shall you serve.'"
Then the devil left him, and behold, angels came and were ministering to him.**

MATTHEW 4:1–11

Jesus followed the Spirit into the wilderness to be tempted by the devil.
The desert trial went on for forty days. After the testing, Jesus was hungry.
Jesus was weakened in every human way during this trial. Satan attacked
him with the promise of food for His physical needs, with validation of His
identity, and with the promise of worldly power. Jesus could have eaten His
fill of fresh bread, been affirmed in His identity, and gained worldly power
with the right responses to Satan.

This was a God-ordained time in the life of Jesus—a time of testing
and allowing the tempter to have access to His Son. Do you think God the
Father loves you any less? Is your temptation a God-ordained time of testing? How have you managed your temptations? Consider documenting
your temptations with room to add how you plan to address these issues.

Jesus consistently responded to these temptations with Scripture. Satan
used emotional and psychological warfare by calling the deity of Christ
into question, asking, if you are the Son of God, do this simple thing that
will benefit you and harm no one. In other words, prove it! Jesus said no.
He would not give in. Even when Satan tried to use Scripture against Jesus,
He would not have it.

Maybe you need to apply a verse of Scripture to your tempter. What passage would you apply to the temptations you have encountered? Consider writing those passages down. Maybe you should memorize a passage for moments of weakness when you least expect a temptation, and you are most vulnerable. Jesus rightly applied the Word of God to temptations the devil is still using against His children. Anticipate the temptations and be prepared to answer with God's Word.

5

Blessed Outcomes

Seeing the crowds, he went up on the mountain, and when he sat down, his disciples came to him. And he opened his mouth and taught them, saying: "Blessed are the poor in spirit, for theirs is the kingdom of heaven. "Blessed are those who mourn, for they shall be comforted. "Blessed are the meek, for they shall inherit the earth. "Blessed are those who hunger and thirst for righteousness, for they shall be satisfied. "Blessed are the merciful, for they shall receive mercy. "Blessed are the pure in heart, for they shall see God. "Blessed are the peacemakers, for they shall be called sons of God. "Blessed are those who are persecuted for righteousness' sake, for theirs is the kingdom of heaven. "Blessed are you when others revile you and persecute youand utter all kinds of evil against you falsely on my account. Rejoice and be glad, for your reward is great in heaven, for so they persecuted the prophets who were before you.

MATTHEW 5:1–12

How often do we read "The Beatitudes" and affirm the goodness of the end product without consideration for the end-producing action? We readily identify with the wonderful results of having the kingdom of Heaven, being comforted, inheriting the earth, being satisfied, receiving mercy, seeing God, and being called sons of God. This is an awesome list: Yes, thank you, and may I have a little more?! However, Jesus described the attitude of these believers first. Do we have the same reaction if we are told that our goal today is the following: become poor in spirit, mourn, be meek, hunger and thirst for righteousness, be merciful, be pure in heart, and be a peacemaker?

Suddenly the outcome seems like a stretch, and the list seems unattainable. Humility comes first. When we desire the outcomes, we are appreciating what is ours in Christ. We will taste and see these outcomes when we abide in Christ. In the process of relating to Jesus, we become more like Him. Becoming more like Him, we will be identified more and more by the attributes ascribed to Him. This is you becoming Christlike—more like Jesus every day.

You can know that you have been identified in Jesus Christ when "others revile you and persecute you and utter all kinds of evil against you falsely on [His] account." Are you there yet? Do you want to be there? Your reward will be great in Heaven. Until then, rejoice and be glad!

There are seven Christlike attitudes to adopt from this passage. Consider writing those seven attitudes down. Ask the Lord to help you with one each day. Lean into a relationship with Jesus and ask Him to show you the way.

6

Deeper Impact

How many times have we crossed this passage and moved on to something we can readily deal with in our lives? Who is actually going to cut off a hand or gouge out their eye over sin? Jesus suggested that "you" should.

If cutting off a specific hand or the eye causing you to sin would stop you from sinning, then this would be an easy solution for anyone serious about dealing with sin in their lives. The hyperbole is here for effect. Sin is *that* serious to the Lord. He wants us to take the matter of sin in our lives *that* seriously.

Sin is not a matter of body parts. Sin is a matter of the heart. Jesus clarifies the original commandment to not commit adultery by saying that His intent was not merely for you to abstain from acts with your body but that He wants your heart focused on Him.

Your heart focused on what you think will please you allows for your eyes to focus on things that align with your heart. If you find that your eyes are wandering and lingering where your heart gets satisfaction from earthly things, you need to check your heart in with the Great Physician who can do heart surgery. Few will admit the sin of adultery; none will deny the sin of lust. Jesus sees them as the same.

Do you need to see the Doctor about your heart? Consider documenting this date as you take your heart in for testing and examination by the only One who can prescribe what you need for cleaning up and preparing your heart as a gift back to the Lord.

7

Goal Setting

**"You have heard that it was said, 'You shall love your neighbor
and hate your enemy.' But I say to you, Love your enemies and
pray for those who persecute you, so that you may be sons of
your Father who is in heaven. For he makes his sun rise on the
evil and on the good, and sends rain on the just and on the
unjust. For if you love those who love you, what reward do
you have? Do not even the tax collectors do the same? And if
you greet only your brothers, what more are you doing than
others? Do not even the Gentiles do the same? You therefore
must be perfect, as your heavenly Father is perfect.**

MATTHEW 5:43–48

We have a tendency to create loopholes for ourselves and then proceed to live in the loophole. Jesus wants us to abide in Him, not a loophole. Given the opportunity to hate anyone, we will find a reason to hate someone. Jesus closes the loophole for us advising that He expects us to love everyone—even those who do not love us back.

Do you *love* anyone like Jesus? Consider making a list of everyone you love. Could you expand that list to include *all* of your family? Could you include your neighbors, even the ones who are not friendly?

How do you love these people? If you were to be convicted of loving them like Jesus, what evidence would the prosecutor bring to the courtroom? Consider writing down the ways in which you currently love your family, your neighbors, and everyone else.

Jesus says to love and pray for those who persecute you. Is this too much to ask? When we find ourselves walking with Christ—trying to identify with Him and busy doing the things that please Him—we will naturally see people as He sees them. Through His eyes we will see people in need of Jesus and love them like He does.

Jesus said we must be perfect. Pursue Jesus and love like Jesus. You move closer to perfection in a relationship with Him.

8

Your Will Be Done

"And when you pray, you must not be like the hypocrites. For they love to stand and pray in the synagogues and at the street corners, that they may be seen by others. Truly, I say to you, they have received their reward. But when you pray, go into your room and shut the door and pray to your Father who is in secret. And your Father who sees in secret will reward you. "And when you pray, do not heap up empty phrases as the Gentiles do, for they think that they will be heard for their many words. Do not be like them, for your Father knows what you need before you ask him. Pray then like this: "Our Father in heaven, hallowed be your name. Your kingdom come, your will be done, on earth as it is in heaven. Give us this day our daily bread, and forgive us our debts, as we also have forgiven our debtors. And lead us not into temptation, but deliver us from evil.

MATTHEW 6:5–13

God has forever insisted that He wants you—not the outward you, or the best you have to offer, or the diversion you create to avoid the real you. God wants you—and not just part of you, the whole you. Jesus wants the you that comes out when no one else is looking. He wants the you available to Him when you are done impressing others. And when you are finished telling God with your mouth what you think He wants to hear, He wants the cry of your heart.

Jesus models for us the base cry of our hearts when we are yielded to Him and interested in hearing from Him. We humbly acknowledge Him on the throne of Heaven, with reverence and fear. We cede our kingdom for His kingdom and welcome Him as the rightful ruler over Heaven and earth. We are so full of Him that all we ask is for what we need in the current day. And we confess our sin—not just the sinful state into which we were born but the specific failures that add to the debt to be forgiven through Christ. The model includes instruction to forgive others baked into the request for our own forgiveness. Finally, Jesus says to pray that you are not led into temptation (even though He was) but that you would be delivered from evil.

How does your prayer life compare to what the Lord asks for and models for us? Do you have a prayer life beyond meals, bedtime, and when you are in a bind?

Can you identify your own heart cry over the words of your prayers? Consider writing down your prayer for today. God already knows what you want and what you need. He wants the time with you. He wants to speak to your heart. Are you in a prayerful posture ready to hear from Him?

9

I Know You

"Not everyone who says to me, 'Lord, Lord,' will enter the kingdom of heaven, but the one who does the will of my Father who is in heaven. On that day many will say to me, 'Lord, Lord, did we not prophesy in your name, and cast out demons in your name, and do many mighty works in your name?' And then will I declare to them, 'I never knew you; depart from me, you workers of lawlessness.'"

MATTHEW 7:21–23

To those who have rightly acknowledged who Jesus is, prophesied in His name, cast out demons, and done mighty works in His name, He reserved some of the harshest words in Scripture: "Depart from me, you workers of lawlessness." Other translations render the words as "evildoers"! This is the day of judgment, and these people have been part of some amazing works in Jesus's name. Jesus Himself, however, says to them: "I never knew you."

Are you prepared to have those words spoken to people who have been around you? Is your mercy meter turned on and tuned in to the fact that there are people around you who know things about Jesus and who may even participate in the wonderful activities He is doing? And yet, they do not *know* Jesus. How many people has the Lord led to you for an introduction to Him? How many will greet you in Heaven with, "Hey, I didn't know you were a Christian—why didn't you tell me?" Their introduction to Jesus was from the person He led them to after you missed the opportunity.

Thank Jesus for the gift of faith and the relationship you are allowed to enjoy. Consider writing your prayer out this week and including Scripture reference as part of a thank offering. Pray, too, for whomever the Lord will bring to you for introduction. Make the most of this opportunity. The obedience to make the introduction is yours—the outcome is His.

10

Hearing vs. Doing

"Everyone then who hears these words of mine and does them will be like a wise man who built his house on the rock. And the rain fell, and the floods came, and the winds blew and beat on that house, but it did not fall, because it had been founded on the rock. And everyone who hears these words of mine and does not do them will be like a foolish man who built his house on the sand. And the rain fell, and the floods came, and the winds blew and beat against that house, and it fell, and great was the fall of it."

MATTHEW 7:24–27

How quick are we to appreciate this passage with self-assurance that our house is built on the rock-solid foundation of Jesus? The alternative, as we know, is a house built on the sand of anything but Jesus. The imagery is easy to conjure, and the lesson from Sunday school is simple to remember. Straight from Scripture, we have the unforgettable and timeless advice: Be like the wise man and build your house on the rock!

Right we are to build our foundation, our hopes, and our future on the solid rock of Jesus Christ. God's Word, from Genesis to Revelation, points to Jesus Christ and salvation through faith alone, by grace alone, in Jesus Christ alone, to the glory of God alone. There is no other means by which we are saved.

This passage, however, points us to the act of listening to God. Listening is distinct from hearing. Both the wise man and the foolish man hear the words of Jesus in the passage. The foolish man, however, does not listen. He does not act upon what he is hearing. His foolishness is not in building a house on the sand—that is the comparison. He is foolish for hearing Jesus but not listening. Upon hearing, he turns to his own way, his own plans, his own will.

The wise man listens to Jesus. Upon hearing the voice of his Savior, he acts in obedience. By comparison, his house is built on rock. And when the floods and winds of life appear, the wise man can rest assured that he has faithfully followed the Lord Jesus. He has no fear of the storms of life.

The storms of life tend to reveal our foundation. How sturdy is your house? Are you listening to the sound of your Savior's voice? What is the last thing you were told to do? Have you obeyed Him? Consider writing down what Jesus is telling you to do, along with an open box to check when you have obeyed.

11

Beware

MATTHEW 10:16–22

What are you prepared to endure today? Or is your day already booked so tight that you will have no time for anything beyond a quick read (this?) and a prayer for everyone to have a good day?

God has placed you where you are today without any natural protection to keep you safe. You may look to the sturdy house He provided, or the new air bag technology in the car He provided, or even to the 401(k) that He has graciously allowed you to maintain. In reality, however, you are like a sheep living among so many wolves. Your outer shell is no match for the teeth of a wolf pack. Your legs will not outrun a wolf, and your fighting skills are not enough.

Jesus has admonished you to be wise. In your wisdom, be aware of what men are prepared to do to you because of your relationship with Jesus. They are like wolves. You will be mistreated and hated, possibly even handed over by family because you stand for Christ.

Enter the Good Shepherd. In your wisdom, put your trust in the Shepherd. Not only are you without natural protection, you have no script to follow or clever escape phrase. Worry not. You will be given what you need to verbally reply to everyone under the guidance of the Holy Spirit. Your job is to follow the Shepherd. Anxiety will distract you from Him.

Jesus also admonished you to be innocent, like a dove. Don't try to bring about the kingdom of God yourself. God is Almighty, not you. You are to be wise and innocent, following the voice of the Shepherd, being obedient to Him. Follow Him like a sheep, and He will take care of the wolves.

Where will the Lord ask you to go today? What will He ask you to do? Are you prepared to defenselessly go in obedience? Are you prepared to do so in wisdom and innocence?

12

Loss of Life

MATTHEW 10:37–39

Jesus demands to be first in your life. Above your love for your parents, above your love for your kids, Jesus wants to be first. If there is anything in your life that you value above your relationship with Him, He will root that out and expose it. The rich young ruler valued his possessions more than knowing Jesus. Maybe there are people in your life who get more time, attention, and loyalty than Christ. What is it that holds such a place in your heart that it would rival your love for the Lord? Consider praying over that question. Make some notes about what the Lord reveals to you as you pray and read this passage this week.

Do you so love the Lord Jesus that you would willingly die for Him? He calls on us to take up our cross and follow Him. The cross is unmistakably an instrument of death. Following Him may not lead to a heinous, torturous death—but it might. If you take up your cross and find your life, you can be sure that you missed the part about following Him. If you take up your cross and find that it changed all your plans, came with hard decisions, and you joyfully acknowledge that you cannot imagine any other life, then you are finding life in Him as He intended.

Will you agree to take up your cross *and* follow Him? Be prepared for family and other competing interests to wail loudly and try aggressively to dissuade you from following Jesus. Putting Jesus first means making hard choices now that will appear easy in hindsight as you live the abundant life He intended for you.

13

From the Heart

Then Peter came up and said to him, "Lord, how often will my brother sin against me, and I forgive him? As many as seven times?" Jesus said to him, "I do not say to you seven times, but seventy-seven times. "Therefore the kingdom of heaven may be compared to a king who wished to settle accounts with his servants. When he began to settle, one was brought to him who owed him ten thousand talents. And since he could not pay, his master ordered him to be sold, with his wife and children and all that he had, and payment to be made. So the servant fell on his knees, imploring him, 'Have patience with me, and I will pay you everything.' And out of pity for him, the master of that servant released him and forgave him the debt. But when that same servant went out, he found one of his fellow servants who owed him a hundred denarii, and seizing him, he began to choke him, saying, 'Pay what you owe.' So his fellow servant fell down and pleaded with him, 'Have patience with me, and I will pay you.' He refused and went and put him in prison until he should pay the debt. When his fellow servants saw what had taken place, they were greatly distressed, and they went and reported to their master all that had taken place. Then his master summoned him and said to him, 'You wicked servant! I forgave you all that debt because you pleaded with me. And should not you have had mercy on your fellow servant, as I had mercy on you?' And in anger his master delivered him to the jailers, until he should pay all his debt. So also my heavenly Father will do to every one of you, if you do not forgive your brother from your heart."

MATTHEW 18:21–35

We can find it easy to get distracted by the numbers. Ask someone you know about this and similar passages, and you will get their thoughts about forgiveness in numerical terms of seventy-seven, or seven times seven, or seventy-seven times seven. I don't think Jesus was advising us to track the numbers, or to configure an end of your willingness to forgive. He immediately told Peter about the kingdom of Heaven where people who were unable to repay debts are forgiven by our Lord and Master.

Here on earth, we look for a way to end our forgiveness, a way to cap our willingness to love one another and be released of the burden of extending ourselves again. Jesus wasn't advising Peter to add numbers to his forgiveness portfolio. He ended the heavenly comparison by advising us to forgive from the heart.

Are you finding the extension of forgiveness to someone difficult? Is there a list of offenses so high, or a hurt that is so deep, that you don't know how to manage forgiveness? Consider writing out where you are struggling. Pray for the right attitude to overtake your heart in favor of forgiveness. Sometimes praying for our own forgiveness (again) helps to soften up the heart toward being able to forgive others where they have offended or hurt us. Pray, too, for insight into just how important our Lord views our heart in forgiving others.

14

Love

But when the Pharisees heard that he had silenced the Sadducees, they gathered together. And one of them, a lawyer, asked him a question to test him. "Teacher, which is the great commandment in the Law?" And he said to him, "You shall love the Lord your God with all your heart and with all your soul and with all your mind. This is the great and first commandment. And a second is like it: You shall love your neighbor as yourself. On these two commandments depend all the Law and the Prophets."

MATTHEW 22:34–40

Jesus sums up the history of the law and the prophets in one word: love. Under the umbrella of love, He includes Himself and all His creation. And in case we are tempted to love with our heads but not our hearts, He makes certain that we understand that this is loving with your whole self.

How are you doing in your quest to love the Lord with your whole heart, soul, and mind? If you are serious about pursuing Him and loving Him, consider making this your prayer this week: "Lord, would you show me where I need to shore up my love for you?" Jesus equated loving Him with obeying Him. Do you need to add this to your prayer? "Lord, help me to understand where I have failed, where I have not been obedient, and where I can love you completely."

The second command is much like the first, but instead of being a vertical love for the Lord your God, this is a horizontal command to love your neighbor. Scripture gives no free pass on who God considers to be your neighbor. We are to love everyone. So how are you doing with loving people in your neighborhood? Do you love them enough to introduce them to Jesus? Just when we think we can check off the box of loving our neighbor "enough," we are reminded to love them as we love ourselves.

Who comes to mind when you are reminded to love your neighbor? Consider making notes about whomever you will be intentional about loving this week.

When we love those whom the Lord brings into our life, even for a moment, we show that we love Him. Be prepared to use words if necessary.

15

Inside Out

"Woe to you, scribes and Pharisees, hypocrites! For you tithe mint and dill and cumin, and have neglected the weightier matters of the law: justice and mercy and faithfulness. These you ought to have done, without neglecting the others. You blind guides, straining out a gnat and swallowing a camel! "Woe to you, scribes and Pharisees, hypocrites! For you clean the outside of the cup and the plate, but inside they are full of greed and self-indulgence. You blind Pharisee! First clean the inside of the cup and the plate, that the outside also may be clean.

MATTHEW 23:23–26

Jesus had some very harsh words for the Pharisees. Would He have any less than a rebuke for you and me? The recipients of the chastisement in this passage did a lot of things right: they tithed, ground out details about their theology and faith, and made sure that all appearances pointed toward their devotion for the Lord. Jesus ripped through all of this because He knew it all came from a corrupted heart. Motives matter to the Lord.

How clean are you on the inside? Only the Lord knows, and He may be trying to get your attention about that. It's not that He does not appreciate the tithes and everything else we may do for Him. But when they are done as a matter for show and tell only, they become offensive to Him. When the inside is not clean, the gift is sullied as well.

Humility leads to repentance. Repentance leads to forgiveness. Get humble before the Lord. Ask the Lord for a look inside your heart. Consider writing down things that He would show you. Pray over insights into justice, mercy, and forgiveness. Are these flowing from you to people in your life? How about greed and self-indulgence? Are these flowing too, or are these bound and captive to Christ?

Lean into the Lord. Pray for a river of goodness to flow from the Lord, through you, into everyone you encounter this week.

16

Why the Hard Heart?

Immediately he made his disciples get into the boat and go before him to the other side, to Bethsaida, while he dismissed the crowd. And after he had taken leave of them, he went up on the mountain to pray. And when evening came, the boat was out on the sea, and he was alone on the land. And he saw that they were making headway painfully, for the wind was against them. And about the fourth watch of the night he came to them, walking on the sea. He meant to pass by them, but when they saw him walking on the sea they thought it was a ghost, and cried out, for they all saw him and were terrified. But immediately he spoke to them and said, "Take heart; it is I. Do not be afraid." And he got into the boat with them, and the wind ceased. And they were utterly astounded, for they did not understand about the loaves, but their hearts were hardened.

MARK 6:45–52

Jesus had just fed an enormous crowd (five thousand men plus) with five loaves of bread and two fish. In the aftermath of feeding the crowd, the disciples gathered up twelve baskets of leftover food. Having not been there nor seen it with your own eyes, do you believe it? The disciples *were* there. They *did* see this with their own eyes.

Hours later, the disciples are in the very boat that Jesus commanded them to take to the other side of the small Sea of Galilee. How odd that they are terrified and crying out at the sight of anything after witnessing the command their Lord has upon the earth, knowing that He told them to be in that boat, crossing that water, where they are now so scared. It's easy to be the Monday morning quarterback on this!

I would likely have been quite taken with the production of a feast on command. What a great trick! He saved the disciples the embarrassment of letting the crowd gather without consideration for their needs, and fed them as well. Would we have wondered or cared about the Lord's purpose in displaying His power? Would we have just been happy to have a meal, reaffirm our standing associated with the Miracle Man, and then looked to see what was next on the agenda? How about a bigger crowd? Maybe some real meat and wine next time?

Jesus patiently continued to work on their hardened hearts with more signs of His deity. He walked to them on top of the water and caused the headwind to cease. What more does Jesus need to show us before we take heart? What does He have to do for us to give up on being afraid? Do we fret over and even fear outcomes that are naturally under His control? Will you trust your God and your Savior to provide everything you need to accomplish what He has asked you to do? The story is here for a reason. Will we repeat the folly of the disciples, or can (should) we learn and grow from the lesson?

Defiled Inside

And he called the people to him again and said to them, "Hear me, all of you, and understand: There is nothing outside a person that by going into him can defile him, but the things that come out of a person are what defile him." And when he had entered the house and left the people, his disciples asked him about the parable. And he said to them, "Then are you also without understanding? Do you not see that whatever goes into a person from outside cannot defile him, since it enters not his heart but his stomach, and is expelled?" (Thus he declared all foods clean.) And he said, "What comes out of a person is what defiles him. For from within, out of the heart of man, come evil thoughts, sexual immorality, theft, murder, adultery, coveting, wickedness, deceit, sensuality, envy, slander, pride, foolishness. All these evil things come from within, and they defile a person."

MARK 7:14–23

Jesus consistently goes after our heart. We, however, consistently offer almost anything but our heart as a substitute. Like that room in our house that we do not want anyone to see, we close the door to our heart and offer diversionary replacements instead of what the Lord requests. We would like to think that if we harshly regulate what we eat, what we watch, and what we listen to that this will be offering enough for the Lord. Meanwhile, Jesus is seeking to occupy a heart that is full of worldly junk. Jesus knows our hearts.

What would we find if your heart was open for inspection? Would the list of defiling offenses from the passage above be complete?

Jesus offers to clean out the heart and occupy that space so that what flows from your heart is clean, honorable, and beneficial to those around you. Are you harboring safe space for junk in your life—space that is off-limits to Christ? Ask for His help admitting and identifying heart-bound things that defile the space reserved for Jesus. Consider documenting your prayer as you seek forgiveness and cleansing. Leave room for documenting the flow of love and righteousness where defiling things used to live.

18

Your Attention Please

On one occasion, while the crowd was pressing in on him to hear the word of God, he was standing by the lake of Gennesaret, and he saw two boats by the lake, but the fishermen had gone out of them and were washing their nets. Getting into one of the boats, which was Simon's, he asked him to put out a little from the land. And he sat down and taught the people from the boat. And when he had finished speaking, he said to Simon, "Put out into the deep and let down your nets for a catch." And Simon answered, "Master, we toiled all night and took nothing! But at your word I will let down the nets." And when they had done this, they enclosed a large number of fish, and their nets were breaking. They signaled to their partners in the other boat to come and help them. And they came and filled both the boats, so that they began to sink. But when Simon Peter saw it, he fell down at Jesus' knees, saying, "Depart from me, for I am a sinful man, O Lord." For he and all who were with him were astonished at the catch of fish that they had taken, and so also were James and John, sons of Zebedee, who were partners with Simon. And Jesus said to Simon, "Do not be afraid; from now on you will be catching men." And when they had brought their boats to land, they left everything and followed him.

LUKE 5:1–11

Jesus could have had two boats full of fish appear out of nowhere. He could have told the fish to swim over and jump into the boats. Instead, Jesus put Himself between Peter and his trusted logic. Peter had already fished all night with no success. Begrudgingly, Peter agreed to row back out and lower the nets. Jesus defies Peter's experience and logic and fills the nets with fish. Now He has Peter's attention. What does the Lord have to do to get *your* attention?

The jubilation must have been quite the spectacle as the second boat is summoned to help with the catch. Peter, however, sees through the miraculous catch to God in the flesh. He bows down to Jesus, confesses his sinful state to the Lord, and begs Jesus to go away that He might not become unclean for having been with a sinful man. Would you have the same reaction as Peter?

Are you in need of a Savior, or is your righteousness enough to get you through this day on your own? You can always deal with the questions of sin, repentance, and forgiveness tomorrow or next week—maybe later, right?

Your posture and humility before the Lord tells Him if you believe you are in need. Jesus knew that Peter was ready for revelation, and He penetrated Peter's defenses in order to get his full attention. Peter clearly did not understand the whole story at this point, but he took the right posture before the Lord with the revelation he was given in this story.

After this amazing miracle, the disciples left everything to follow Jesus. They left their boats, the miraculous catch, the nets, and their hope for a payday to wisely follow the One who provided all these things. What does the Lord have your attention about right now? Consider making some notes about what He is conveying to you. Is He also asking you to leave it all to follow Him to something new?

19

The Word God

In the beginning was the Word, and the Word was with God, and the Word was God. He was in the beginning with God. All things were made through him, and without him was not any thing made that was made. In him was life, and the life was the light of men. The light shines in the darkness, and the darkness has not overcome it. There was a man sent from God, whose name was John. He came as a witness, to bear witness about the light, that all might believe through him. He was not the light, but came to bear witness about the light. The true light, which gives light to everyone, was coming into the world. He was in the world, and the world was made through him, yet the world did not know him. He came to his own, and his own people did not receive him. But to all who did receive him, who believed in his name, he gave the right to become children of God, who were born, not of blood nor of the will of the fleshnor of the will of man, but of God.

JOHN 1:1–13

Jesus, aka the Word, was with God the Father and God the Spirit in the beginning. Jesus was not part of the creation; He was part of the Creator. All creation was made through the Word. In the Word is life, the light of mankind. And yet, when the Word took on flesh and came to earth, we did not recognize Him. He took on human form, was given a common name for the time, and was born to common earthly parents. According to the plans of the Father, Jesus inconspicuously came forth onto the planet He created, through a young girl who was engaged to a common carpenter. The best they could do for their son, the Creator King, Savior of the world, was birth Him in a barn and lay Him in a trough.

How would you have written this story if you were the Lord? The story gets much worse as Jesus sets out to reveal Himself to the world He created and came to save. He performed miracle after miracle, healing the sick, the blind, the lame, and even raising people from the dead. So naturally, He was brought up on charges, arrested, tortured, and executed. The Creator God of all was mocked, beaten, and crucified. Jesus willingly allowed this to happen. And after being laid in a tomb Friday evening, He got up and walked out of the tomb Sunday morning. After appearing to many, He ascended into Heaven and claims to be preparing a place for us right now.

If you believe this wild story, it is because the gift of faith has been granted to you. You were not born with the gift. You could not, and did not, earn the gift. And no amount of wanting the gift causes the Giver to grant you the gift. God's will is for you to use the faith you have to believe this story and *live* your life back to the Lord in daily thanks for this uncommon love.

20

Love One Another

**A new commandment I give to you, that you love one another:
just as I have loved you, you also are to love one another.**

JOHN 13:34

The command to love one another is agreeable, uncontroversial, and nice. Of course, we *love* one another. We always think the best thoughts about one another and assume the best motives about one another. We go out of our way to show love to one another. We even keep some of our assets and resources on standby to show love to someone in need. Our "love one another" box is checked.

Now let's look at how we are *actually* to love one another. Jesus gave the command without many specifics but with Himself as the example: "just as I have loved you." How did Jesus love His disciples? What examples can you think of where Jesus demonstrated His love for people? Consider starting a list of the ways Jesus showed His love.

Jesus loved extravagantly. He crossed geographical borders, religious barriers, ethnic and gender traditions. He loved the diseased and unclean, the rich and poor alike, even showing love to the Roman oppressors. He crossed lines to show love. At the same time, He always told the truth. Where He encountered false teaching, bad theology, sin, and lies, He called them out. He loved people enough to tell them the truth. Jesus knew that the truth would hurt but that He provided the ultimate healing.

On the cross, Jesus showed the ultimate love: taking the punishment we deserved and enduring it Himself. Greater love has never been demonstrated. With the example of Jesus before you, do you need to consider the commandment in a fresh light? Is it time to review the expectations you have set for yourself in obeying this commandment?

21

Keep It Simple

If you love me, you will keep my commandments.

JOHN 14:15

Jesus has a habit of simplifying. People have a habit of complicating. Have you complicated this simple passage in your walk with Jesus? What does it mean to love Jesus and therefore be obedient to His commands? Do you obey Him because you love Him or love Him by obeying Him—or maybe both?

All at one time, Jesus is our friend, brother, teacher, savior, and the Son of God. In each of these roles, Jesus loves us first. He paid the unthinkable penalty for a relationship to be possible with us. His love for us is never-ending. Our response to this undeserved, unfathomable love is what? What is your response when asked if you love Jesus? Consider writing a response to this question.

There are many ways to gauge your love for Jesus. God alone is the judge, but maybe it is helpful to think about how it is that we love our Savior. The Lord loves honesty, integrity, sacrificial giving, and time with you. The hallmark of loving Jesus, however, is to do what He commanded. In obedience to His commands, you are found guilty of loving Him.

How are you doing with your obedience to Him? Recall that Jesus summed up the law and the prophets with one word: love. By loving the Lord your God and loving your neighbor as yourself, we are fulfilling the commands of Christ. Love God first, people second.

If you have complicated this command to the point of not obeying, give that confession to the Lord this week. Ask for insight on how to obey the command to love. Be prepared for God to give you new opportunities to show the love of Jesus to people.

22

Plugged In

**"I am the true vine, and my Father is the vinedresser. Every branch
in me that does not bear fruit he takes away, and every branch that
does bear fruit he prunes, that it may bear more fruit. Already you
are clean because of the word that I have spoken to you. Abide in
me, and I in you. As the branch cannot bear fruit by itself, unless it
abides in the vine, neither can you, unless you abide in me. I am the
vine; you are the branches. Whoever abides in me and I in him, he
it is that bears much fruit, for apart from me you can do nothing.
If anyone does not abide in me he is thrown away like a branch
and withers; and the branches are gathered, thrown into the fire,
and burned. If you abide in me, and my words abide in you, ask
whatever you wish, and it will be done for you. By this my Father is
glorified, that you bear much fruit and so prove to be my disciples.**

JOHN 15:1–8

Jesus takes an earthly reality to help His disciples understand a heavenly concept. The disciples would have been very familiar with grapevines. The care and maintenance of a grapevine would have been easy for them to quickly grasp. The fruit of the grapevine is, of course, clumps of grapes. Even without personal experience caring for grapes, we can appreciate that there is going to be a spectrum of success for various vines. Their success depends on many factors: soil, sunlight, water, and external impacts such as storms, animals, and humans.

The goal for any grapevine manager is to grow grapes—lots of healthy grapes. The grapes in this passage are the fruit that you bear in your relationship with Jesus Christ. Jesus is the overall vine, we are the branches, and the fruit—the end product—is the good works we do in His name. How healthy and robust is the fruit you are bearing in your life?

God the Father is the vinedresser, the caretaker, and the judge who determines how best to maintain the vine. If He is pleased with the fruit coming from certain branches, maybe He will seek to ensure that this branch gets even more nutrition from the vine. Other branches will be cut off for lack of production.

Jesus does not admonish you to try harder to produce much fruit. He says that the branches are to abide in Him. The more nutrition we get directly from the Source, the more fruit is likely to result from our branch. Jesus says that even the good branch will be pruned in order to make it more productive. Lean into Jesus, expect pruning, and ask the Lord for the ability to be faithful to Him. The fruit will follow.

23

Restoration

When they had finished breakfast, Jesus said to Simon Peter, "Simon, son of John, do you love me more than these?" He said to him, "Yes, Lord; you know that I love you." He said to him, "Feed my lambs." He said to him a second time, "Simon, son of John, do you love me?" He said to him, "Yes, Lord; you know that I love you." He said to him, "Tend my sheep." He said to him the third time, "Simon, son of John, do you love me?" Peter was grieved because he said to him the third time, "Do you love me?" and he said to him, "Lord, you know everything; you know that I love you." Jesus said to him, "Feed my sheep. Truly, truly, I say to you, when you were young, you used to dress yourself and walk wherever you wanted, but when you are old, you will stretch out your hands, and another will dress you and carry you where you do not want to go." (This he said to show by what kind of death he was to glorify God.) And after saying this he said to him, "Follow me."

JOHN 21:15–19

Peter was grieved after the Lord repeated His question a third time. Peter was the first to acknowledge Jesus as the Christ and the only one recorded to have drawn a sword to keep Jesus from being arrested. Peter had also been advised that although he was correct about who Jesus was, his confidence would give way to fear on the night Jesus was arrested, as he denied even knowing Jesus three times. I wonder if Peter realized what Jesus was accomplishing in that moment, or how long it took for the reality of His provision to settle in his mind.

Jesus took the time to restore Peter to Himself through a somewhat humiliating process of walking back the denials and replacing them with affirmations of his love. Jesus was preparing Peter for his ministry of care—tending to the flock and providing them with the Gospel. Jesus was apparently also preparing Peter for the difficult road he was being asked to walk. Ultimately, regardless of the details, Peter was told to follow Jesus.

Has the Lord attempted to restore you to Himself in some way? Does He keep asking you the same question? Maybe you are encountering the same problem, or things just seem to keep turning out the same way? Consider these questions in spiritual terms and open yourself up to the possibility that the Great Healer is attempting to heal a wound that has persisted without your attention until now. Jesus asked an imperfect believer to feed His sheep and follow Him. Would He expect or ask any less of you?

24

Uncommon Boldness

**Then Peter, filled with the Holy Spirit, said to them, "Rulers of
the people and elders, if we are being examined today concerning
a good deed done to a crippled man, by what means this man
has been healed, let it be known to all of you and to all the
people of Israel that by the name of Jesus Christ of Nazareth,
whom you crucified, whom God raised from the dead—by him
this man is standing before you well. This Jesus is the stone
that was rejected by you, the builders, which has become the
cornerstone. And there is salvation in no one else, for there is no
other name under heaven given among men by which we must be
saved." Now when they saw the boldness of Peter and John, and
perceived that they were uneducated, common men, they were
astonished. And they recognized that they had been with Jesus.**

ACTS 4:8–13

Peter and John were bold. Common, uneducated men, their speech *astonished* the Jewish leaders. Did Peter have a rehearsed recipe for astonishing his audience? Maybe a tight, vetted theological masterpiece to roll out on the people? No.

The Word says that Peter was filled with the Holy Spirit. Out of the overflow of his heart, the Holy Spirit simply laid out the truth from the mouth of an ordinary fisherman.

Peter was boldly used by God to proclaim the truth that Jesus Christ was crucified for our salvation and raised from the dead that we may know life. Through Jesus, the blind will see, the lame will walk, and the dead will also rise. There is salvation in no other way.

Peter, who had no formal training or skills, other than fishing, made himself available to the Lord. God used a fisherman to fish for people. How might the Lord be able to use you? Are you focused more on the content of a script or on the Spirit who will speak through you? The religious leaders recognized that Peter and John had been with Jesus. Do people recognize that you have been with Jesus? Consider spending time this week praying over the simple truth of the Gospel. Maybe write down how and where you fit in the Gospel story. The Holy Spirit filled a common laborer to the point that he astonished the unlikely audience he held. Are you prepared to be used by the Lord?

25

Obey God or Man?

And when they had brought them, they set them before the council. And the high priest questioned them, saying, "We strictly charged you not to teach in this name, yet here you have filled Jerusalem with your teaching, and you intend to bring this man's blood upon us." But Peter and the apostles answered, "We must obey God rather than men. The God of our fathers raised Jesus, whom you killed by hanging him on a tree. God exalted him at his right hand as Leader and Savior, to give repentance to Israel and forgiveness of sins. And we are witnesses to these things, and so is the Holy Spirit, whom God has given to those who obey him."

ACTS 5:27–32

There will likely come a time when you will be challenged to speak only what is approved by man. Maybe we are already there, and you have been silenced from saying anything that could be construed as offensive. Are you silent when you know you should speak?

Make no mistake, God does not need you to speak for Him. He could have the truth spoken by other followers, even children. And if we do not speak, God can cause the rocks, trees, and wind to speak. That's not an issue for the Lord. The question is not one of speeches. The question is around obedience. If you are led to speak and do not, you are not being obedient.

Peter and the apostles had been witnesses to the resurrection of Jesus Christ. They were simply telling the truth about what they had witnessed. You, too, can be a witness for what you have seen in your life. The government, the employers, and the ruling mob may request or even require your public silence on spiritual matters. You must obey God.

If God leads you to speak, tell your story. Tell them about the transformation in your own life. Consider writing out your story this week. Tell them about the hope you live with and the abundant life that exists because of that hope. Worldly authorities and powers will continue to seek your silence about the Savior. Peter, later in life, advised us to always be prepared to answer everyone who asks you for the reason for the hope you have and to do this with gentleness and respect (1 Peter 3:15). Be prepared to speak the truth with love. Trust the Lord to provide the timing and the words. Your job is to be obedient. The battle is the Lord's.

26

Actual Truth

**If you say, "Behold, we did not know this," does not he who weighs
the heart perceive it? Does not he who keeps watch over your
soul know it, and will he not repay man according to his work?**

PROVERBS 24:12

Do you have a problem telling the truth—the whole truth? Or maybe you
are good at engineering conversations to avoid having to tell the truth? If
this is you, consider making notes to that effect. Turn those notes into a
prayer of confession. Upon that confession, speak the truth.

There are others, maybe you can identify, who speak true words but are
intentionally leading people to a false conclusion. This practice is common
enough among mankind to garner a place in the dictionary: paltering.

God does not get fooled, and it doesn't take long for the people
around you to catch on to falsehood either. God has a huge advantage. He
knows your heart. He sifts the heart, weighs the heart, and understands
the motives driving your heart. Why do we continue pretending like He
doesn't exist—or that He does exist but doesn't pay attention to these
details? He does.

God even tests your heart. He tests for genuineness and faithfulness.
When we lie to and manipulate people, we are putting the test back on the
Lord. We are testing His willingness to discipline and correct His children.
As a believer in the Lord Jesus Christ, as one under the covenant of His
blood, and one to whom all the promises have been given, you are held to
the highest possible standard. Your yes should be *Yes* and your no should
be *No*. Out of the overflow of your redeemed heart should flow rivers of
truth and love.

27

Free at Last

About midnight Paul and Silas were praying and singing hymns to God, and the prisoners were listening to them, and suddenly there was a great earthquake, so that the foundations of the prison were shaken. And immediately all the doors were opened, and everyone's bonds were unfastened. When the jailer woke and saw that the prison doors were open, he drew his sword and was about to kill himself, supposing that the prisoners had escaped. But Paul cried with a loud voice, "Do not harm yourself, for we are all here." And the jailer called for lights and rushed in, and trembling with fear he fell down before Paul and Silas. Then he brought them out and said, "Sirs, what must I do to be saved?" And they said, "Believe in the Lord Jesus, and you will be saved, you and your household." And they spoke the word of the Lord to him and to all who were in his house. And he took them the same hour of the night and washed their wounds; and he was baptized at once, he and all his family. Then he brought them up into his house and set food before them. And he rejoiced along with his entire household that he had believed in God.

ACTS 16:25–34

Between the lines of this passage, we see that it was pitch dark at midnight in the prison. Paul and Silas are praying and singing, despite their circumstances. Their music and speech have put the jailer to sleep, but other prisoners are listening to them. There is suddenly a great earthquake. The prison doors open, and the prison shackles fall off the hands and feet of the prisoners. None of the prisoners move. In the dark, the jailer can now see that the doors are open, so he assumes the worst. If the prisoners are gone, he is responsible. He draws his sword to carry out an inevitable death sentence upon himself. The prisoners, however, have not escaped. Despite being freed of their bonds, they remain. Paul assures the prison guard, who calls for lanterns to confirm that this is true.

In a few moments of time, the prison guard goes from wanting to kill himself to wanting to be saved. He recognizes from the praying, singing, and unnatural response to being freed that Paul and Silas have something that he does not: assurance of salvation. The jailer and his whole household were baptized that night! In his new boldness, the jailer even showed these guys the kindness of cleaning their wounds and feeding them in his house.

When you have been dealt a crummy deal, like Paul and Silas, do you respond with prayer and singing? Would your reaction to life's circumstances be looked upon by nonbelievers with desire to possess what you possess? Nonbelievers are watching to see how you handle difficulty. Is there something different about you?

28

Live by Faith

First, I thank my God through Jesus Christ for all of you, because your faith is proclaimed in all the world. For God is my witness, whom I serve with my spirit in the gospel of his Son, that without ceasing I mention you always in my prayers, asking that somehow by God's will I may now at last succeed in coming to you. For I long to see you, that I may impart to you some spiritual gift to strengthen you—that is, that we may be mutually encouraged by each other's faith, both yours and mine. I do not want you to be unaware, brothers, that I have often intended to come to you (but thus far have been prevented), in order that I may reap some harvest among you as well as among the rest of the Gentiles. I am under obligation both to Greeks and to barbarians, both to the wise and to the foolish. So I am eager to preach the gospel to you also who are in Rome. For I am not ashamed of the gospel, for it is the power of God for salvation to everyone who believes, to the Jew first and also to the Greek. For in it the righteousness of God is revealed from faith for faith, as it is written, "The righteous shall live by faith."

ROMANS 1:8–17

The faith of the believers in Rome was being proclaimed all over the known world. Paul desperately wanted to get to Rome, to be with these believers. He wanted to preach the Gospel there and exchange encouragement with the believers. He had put in the time praying for these folks; now he wanted to be with them in person. Do we have the same drive to share the Gospel and be present with other believers?

Paul had an amazing focus on making the Gospel known. Paul would share the Gospel with anyone, anywhere, any time. He would share his faith with prison guards, political authorities, religious authorities, and outcasts. Paul had no fear and no shame. He challenged pillars in the church (Peter, in particular), and crossed the cultural, political, and religious lines to proclaim the truth to anyone who would listen (and probably some who wouldn't listen). Possessing the same good news, having the same faith, knowing the same Savior, why do we lack the same confidence and zeal?

The Gospel of Jesus Christ is the power of God. The Gospel is the power conduit for salvation. Sharing that power, the power alive in you, should be a natural exercise. We should be willing and ready, even eager, to share this truth. Who is the last person you shared the truth of your life with? Pray for an opportunity for the Lord to use you today.

29

Guard Your Heart

My son, be attentive to my words; incline your ear to my sayings. Let them not escape from your sight; keep them within your heart. For they are life to those who find them, and healing to all their flesh. Keep your heart with all vigilance, for from it flow the springs of life. Put away from you crooked speech, and put devious talk far from you. Let your eyes look directly forward, and your gaze be straight before you. Ponder the path of your feet; then all your ways will be sure. Do not swerve to the right or to the left; turn your foot away from evil.

PROVERBS 4:20–27

In *Cheating Death*, I dedicated a whole chapter to the central sentence of this passage, which in the NIV says: "Above all else, guard your heart, for everything you do flows from it." The great importance of what Solomon was about to reveal could not be overstated, and the wisest man who ever lived says to guard this truth for life and healing.

Who you are, what you say, and what you do—all of this flows, emanates from, and originates in your heart. If your heart is unguarded, you are vulnerable. If you are not taking intentional steps in vigilant defense of your heart, you will be compromised. What are some ways you are intentionally defending your heart? Consider making a list of defensive tactics you are using and share that list with a friend. Maybe we could learn from one another about best and most current practices in guarding our hearts.

To be sure, if the overflow of your heart results in speech that has to be adjusted depending on the audience, you are losing the battle on that front. If your pastor cannot shoulder-surf as you peruse the internet this week, you are compromised on that front as well. And if you are going places you don't need to be going, stop. Guarding your heart is meaningless if you are just going to go places where you are defeated upon arrival. Take steps now to ensure that your heart is protected and the dwelling place of the Holy Spirit is allowed to thrive.

30

More Than Conqueror

What then shall we say to these things? If God is for us, who can be against us? He who did not spare his own Son but gave him up for us all, how will he not also with him graciously give us all things? Who shall bring any charge against God's elect? It is God who justifies. Who is to condemn? Christ Jesus is the one who died—more than that, who was raised—who is at the right hand of God, who indeed is interceding for us. Who shall separate us from the love of Christ? Shall tribulation, or distress, or persecution, or famine, or nakedness, or danger, or sword? As it is written, "For your sake we are being killed all the day long; we are regarded as sheep to be slaughtered." No, in all these things we are more than conquerors through him who loved us. For I am sure that neither death nor life, nor angels nor rulers, nor things present nor things to come, nor powers, nor height nor depth, nor anything else in all creation, will be able to separate us from the love of God in Christ Jesus our Lord.

ROMANS 8:31–39

Is your devotion to the Lord dependent on your circumstances? Scripture tells you exactly how all of this is going to turn out and provides you with a promise to help you until the very end. The conclusion is that God loves you, and through Him you will conquer and overcome everything this world throws at you. You will, in fact, be successful beyond that: *more than conquerors*. With the conclusion determined, the Lord promises that nothing on earth will be able to separate you from the love of God. Nothing. Nothing past, present, or future will be able to take you away from the Lord's good grasp.

Do we fear people, governments, demons, financial crisis? Consider writing down those things that come to mind when you think about what gives you pause (fear). Did Paul leave a small loophole in his list that has you concerned that maybe the love of God in Christ Jesus our Lord just won't cover? Is there unconfessed sin that creates doubt in your heart about the sufficiency of the sacrifice made for you? God is *for* you. He made an enormous sacrifice to claim you as His own. Maybe it is time to begin living like we believe that truth.

God does *not* promise that you will be spared any trial, persecution, or danger. He promises that you will be able to overcome these things through Christ and that these things will not be able to separate you from Him. Jesus is interceding for you right now. Take these questions and issues to Him in prayer. Walk in the promises knowing victory in Him is yours.

31

Good News

**For the Scripture says, "Everyone who believes in him will not
be put to shame." For there is no distinction between Jew and
Greek; for the same Lord is Lord of all, bestowing his riches on all
who call on him. For "everyone who calls on the name of the Lord
will be saved." How then will they call on him in whom they have
not believed? And how are they to believe in him of whom they
have never heard? And how are they to hear without someone
preaching? And how are they to preach unless they are sent? As
it is written, "How beautiful are the feet of those who preach the
good news!" But they have not all obeyed the gospel. For Isaiah
says, "Lord, who has believed what he has heard from us?" So faith
comes from hearing, and hearing through the word of Christ.**

ROMANS 10:11–17

The formula for the salvation of people is pretty straightforward: the Son of God was the blood sacrifice for the sins of people; people with faith in the Son of God have a path to the Lord and the promise of everlasting life with Him in Heaven. That is the plan. People hear the truth, by faith believe the truth, and enjoy an eternal relationship with the Lord.

What Paul is describing here is not a logistics issue. The issue is one of obedience. If nobody was obedient to the command to go tell the Gospel story, would that preclude people from faith and salvation? The Lord could appear Himself and tell people the truth. He could also speak through rocks, animals, or the wind—I don't think He is limited. He does, however, seem to prefer to speak through faithful followers a majority of the time.

Are you faithful and obedient in your calling? Are you involved in sending and preaching the good news of Jesus Christ? Is your faithfulness relegated to giving financial support?

Consider making a list of ways you could be involved in preaching or sending. The truth may not need to be flown halfway around the world and then walked to a remote village. The next presentation of the truth may be at the house next door, or at the office this week, or on the plane to where you are headed tomorrow. Pray and prepare for your next opportunity to speak the truth in love. Your preparation will be met with opportunity.

32

Transformed vs. Conformed

**I appeal to you therefore, brothers, by the mercies of
God, to present your bodies as a living sacrifice, holy and
acceptable to God, which is your spiritual worship. Do not be
conformed to this world, but be transformed by the renewal
of your mind, that by testing you may discern what is the
will of God, what is good and acceptable and perfect.**

ROMANS 12:1–2

God has a good, perfect, and pleasing will for you. Are you in tune with His will for your life? Consider writing out what God's will is for you. If you find that your list is short on details, worry not. You may not even be ready for the revelation of all the details. Let's get ready.

God's will is perfect, specific, and discernable. We are in a position to discern His will when our mind is in a process of renewal. Your mind on God's Word is part of how He will renew your mind.

We have to allow God to transform us from our sinful tendency to conform to the pattern of this world. God's will is discernable with a renewed mind. That renewed mind, that godly perspective, will allow you to be transformed by God. To what end? The goal of being transformed is that we would be in the spiritual worship of our Lord. We do this by offering ourselves as a living sacrifice. In the past, we would offer a sacrifice that had to die. Jesus took that role for us, becoming the ultimate sacrifice, that we might live as a sacrifice for Him. We don't have to die for Him. We get to live for Him.

God's good, acceptable, and perfect will for you is that you would live your life as a sacrifice unto Him. All other aspects of His perfect will for you will be in line with this overall will.

33

Weak Faith Quarrels

As for the one who is weak in faith, welcome him, but not to quarrel over opinions. One person believes he may eat anything, while the weak person eats only vegetables. Let not the one who eats despise the one who abstains, and let not the one who abstains pass judgment on the one who eats, for God has welcomed him. Who are you to pass judgment on the servant of another? It is before his own master that he stands or falls. And he will be upheld, for the Lord is able to make him stand. One person esteems one day as better than another, while another esteems all days alike. Each one should be fully convinced in his own mind. The one who observes the day, observes it in honor of the Lord. The one who eats, eats in honor of the Lord, since he gives thanks to God, while the one who abstains, abstains in honor of the Lord and gives thanks to God. For none of us lives to himself, and none of us dies to himself. For if we live, we live to the Lord, and if we die, we die to the Lord. So then, whether we live or whether we die, we are the Lord's.

ROMANS 14:1–8

How are your relationships within the body of Christ—within your family, your church, the circles you maintain, or the body of believers in your neighborhood? There are so many differences in tradition, practices, and beliefs within our own broad family, so many divisions based on debatable questions of practice. They can be a distraction from the united worship of the One True God.

Are you part of the problem? Do you support the divisions where they rest on disputable matters of custom and tradition? Are you convinced in your own mind that your own custom is right for you in your relationship with the Lord—and that it is okay for your neighbor to practice a different tradition, fully convinced in his mind, within his relationship with the Lord? Could you both be wrong? Is either one based squarely on Scripture or more of a tradition or custom supported by Scripture?

We are advised to not hate or pass judgement on our brothers and sisters in Christ. We will all answer for our actions and our attitudes. Make sure the Lord is good with your sacrifice before you go advising your neighbor on theirs.

34

Christ Confirmed in You

Paul, called by the will of God to be an apostle of Christ Jesus, and our brother Sosthenes, To the church of God that is in Corinth, to those sanctified in Christ Jesus, called to be saints together with all those who in every place call upon the name of our Lord Jesus Christ, both their Lord and ours: Grace to you and peace from God our Father and the Lord Jesus Christ. I give thanks to my God always for you because of the grace of God that was given you in Christ Jesus, that in every way you were enriched in him in all speech and all knowledge—even as the testimony about Christ was confirmed among you—so that you are not lacking in any gift, as you wait for the revealing of our Lord Jesus Christ, who will sustain you to the end, guiltless in the day of our Lord Jesus Christ. God is faithful, by whom you were called into the fellowship of his Son, Jesus Christ our Lord.

1 CORINTHIANS 1:1–9

In this passage, Paul confirms many things about the grace of the Lord, the working of His provision, and the path to the end. He confirms that the Corinthians are set aside (sanctified) in Christ Jesus and called to be saints (along with us). He offers grace and peace from God the Father and the Lord Jesus Christ. He acknowledges that they have been given grace in speech and in knowledge as Paul's testimony was confirmed in them. He even assures them that they have every spiritual gift they need to carry out the mission they were given.

In the end, however, Paul points to the heartbeat of the Corinthian church. Their passion was for the revelation of our Lord Jesus Christ. Is that our heartbeat? Do we long to see the return of Jesus, or is that an afterthought in the smorgasbord of our thought life? The Corinthian church did not get everything right all the time, but they were moving in the right direction. Paul promised that they would be sustained to the end by their faithful God. You were called into this same fellowship. Do you need to make any adjustments?

35

Whose Body?

Flee from sexual immorality. Every other sin a person commits is outside the body, but the sexually immoral person sins against his own body. Or do you not know that your body is a temple of the Holy Spirit within you, whom you have from God? You are not your own, for you were bought with a price. So glorify God in your body.

1 CORINTHIANS 6:18–20

There's not much wiggle room in God's standard on sexual immorality. If you are looking for wiggle room, or an exception to the rule, you are likely on your way to defeat in the battle against sexual immorality.

The command is not given toward the goal of harshness with the body or keeping us from enjoying ourselves. God created sex and made it to be very enjoyable. And, as with every good gift, there is responsibility. This gift was not designed to be opened except within the context of marriage. Opening the gift before God intended you to comes with consequences. Still not convinced? Simply remove this passage and every other passage in the Bible that offends you. Rip those pages out of the Bible and call it whatever you deem appropriate. Hopefully you are not doing that, but there are plenty who are doing just that.

We cannot change the Word of God. You were bought and paid for at a very high price, and God desires a relationship with you. You are not your own. Within you is the temple of the Holy Spirit. Sexual immorality does not belong in, or near, the temple of God.

We are told to stand and fight many times in the Bible. When it comes to sexual impurity, we are told to flee. Guard your heart! Protect yourself from even a hint of sexual immorality. You are expected to glorify God with your body. This includes your eyes, your brain, and every other part of you. Confess what needs confessing. Make a plan to protect the temple.

36

In Love

**Be watchful, stand firm in the faith, act like men,
be strong. Let all that you do be done in love.**

1 CORINTHIANS 16:13–14

How easy it is to interpret this passage with a nod to bravado and come to an illogical conclusion. The admonishment to *act like men* is likely a contrast with the Corinthian proclivity to behave more like juveniles versus acting like women. Accountability and acceptance of responsibility are still attributes of maturity that we find in scarce supply.

Are you watchful for the return of Christ, perhaps also vigilant in protecting yourself from encroaching forms of worldly evil? Paul laid out the full armor of God in Ephesians, chapter six—and with that armor in place, we are to stand. If your faith does not drive your decisions and lead you to take a stand in this world, then you are out of step with your Savior. Faith should enable you to stand firm. Joshua was commanded to be strong. The expectation for followers has not changed. Obedience, and resulting strength, is your faith in action.

The illogical conclusion is that any or all of this passage speaks to guys expressing manliness in human feats of strength and personal resilience. Everything we do is to be done in love. Be lovingly watchful, standing lovingly assured in your faith, submitted in love and willingly accountable, and lovingly strong in all your pursuits of the Lord Jesus Christ.

How would you rate yourself on the five charges from this passage? Consider listing ways you would like to see more depth in these areas.

37

Spiritual Warfare

For though we walk in the flesh, we are not waging war according to the flesh. For the weapons of our warfare are not of the flesh but have divine power to destroy strongholds. We destroy arguments and every lofty opinion raised against the knowledge of God, and take every thought captive to obey Christ.

1 CORINTHIANS 10:3–5

Spiritual warfare is very real. Scripture identifies spiritual warfare and helps us understand how we are to engage. Scripture tells us plainly that this is different than a physical battle. With physical battles in the flesh, we are much more in tune with how to win the fight. We do not like or tolerate discomfort in our flesh and spend a great deal of time and energy making ourselves comfortable in the flesh. If we were literally dealing with the effects of a fleshly battle, the casualties, wounds, and injuries that accompany physical war, we would be much quicker to identify the conflict and get the assistance we need.

If you were awakened this day to mortal conflict going on close to you, would you engage the enemy by yourself? If you could call up a military special forces team to wage war with/for you, wouldn't you do that instead of going into battle alone? Would you try to manage your own wounds while under attack in the flesh? You would be advised against being the lone wolf hero by combat veterans and first responders.

The Bible says this battle is not in the flesh. You cannot call up special weapons operators for help with this battle. Even better, you can call upon the Creator. Not every battle in your life is spiritual warfare. Regardless of the conflict source, you can turn to the Source for help in confidence.

God will supply you with weapons. The weapons you have at your disposal have divine power to win battles. These spiritual battles are designed to keep you from the knowledge of God. Lean into Jesus. Ask Him to cover you and help you take captive every thought and make it obedient to Christ. This is the battleground, and He is the answer to every problem.

38

Spiritual Fruit

**Now the works of the flesh are evident: sexual immorality,
impurity, sensuality, idolatry, sorcery, enmity, strife, jealousy,
fits of anger, rivalries, dissensions, divisions, envy, drunkenness,
orgies, and things like these. I warn you, as I warned you before,
that those who do such things will not inherit the kingdom
of God. But the fruit of the Spirit is love, joy, peace, patience,
kindness, goodness, faithfulness, gentleness, self-control; against
such things there is no law. And those who belong to Christ
Jesus have crucified the flesh with its passions and desires. If
we live by the Spirit, let us also keep in step with the Spirit.**

GALATIANS 5:19–25

Paul uses the word "Spirit" three times in this passage. If you knew nothing more about the Holy Spirit, you would be able to discern from this passage alone that we can live by the Spirit, that the Spirit is moving, and that the Spirit, by analogy, produces fruit. We can also see that the contrast to the Spirit is us in the flesh. And in the contrast, we do not fare well.

Living in the flesh, we produce things consistent with our sinful nature and things opposed to a relationship with the Lord. In many churches today, we are led to believe that we can produce these kinds of works in the flesh and still inherit the kingdom of God. Scripture says otherwise. Our flesh would like to dictate that we can profess faith in Christ and lead a life devoid of a relationship with Him. Again, Scripture clearly and consistently denies the prospect of the eternal coexistence of truth and lies.

For the follower of Jesus Christ, the kingdom of Heaven has already begun. An eternal relationship with the Triune God of the Bible begins with faith. The relationship is eternal. Physical death is simply a change in logistics for the Christian. Love, joy, peace, patience,

kindness, goodness, faithfulness, gentleness, and self-control are the fruit of the Spirit in the life of a believer here and now.

Consider an assessment of your heart and the fruit being produced through you right now. Would the fruit in your life be passed over at the grocery store? Chances are, that is the "fruit" of the flesh, not of the Holy Spirit. Let's live by the Spirit and see His fruit produced in our lives.

39

While You Were Dead

And you were dead in the trespasses and sins in which you once walked, following the course of this world, following the prince of the power of the air, the spirit that is now at work in the sons of disobedience—among whom we all once lived in the passions of our flesh, carrying out the desires of the body and the mind, and were by nature children of wrath, like the rest of mankind. But God, being rich in mercy, because of the great love with which he loved us, even when we were dead in our trespasses, made us alive together with Christ—by grace you have been saved—and raised us up with him and seated us with him in the heavenly places in Christ Jesus, so that in the coming ages he might show the immeasurable riches of his grace in kindness toward us in Christ Jesus. For by grace you have been saved through faith. And this is not your own doing; it is the gift of God, not a result of works, so that no one may boast. For we are his workmanship, created in Christ Jesus for good works, which God prepared beforehand, that we should walk in them.

EPHESIANS 2:1–10

Unless you are super familiar with this passage, I suggest you read it again, very slowly. The problem for most is the part about us being *dead* in our trespasses and sins. Twice Paul uses the words "dead in your trespasses" (sin). How many times have we glossed over this and not beheld the gravity of what Paul is trying to convey?

Imagine trying to give a gift or an award to someone who is dead. Now imagine that the award-giver actually expected the recipient to get up out of the grave, accept the gift, and get to work! You are, or were, the dead party. And the gift is eternal life. You did not earn that gift. How could you? Dead people do nothing but lie dead. So why do we give ourselves any credit for any part of this gifting transaction? And why do we teach kids the same?

You and I were raised from the death we deserved and made alive in Jesus Christ. You did nothing. You were powerless, unable, unwilling, and dead to God. All praise be to the Lord Jesus Christ for the immeasurable riches of His grace in kindness to us. The gift is so undeserved. The Giver is loving beyond our ability to comprehend.

What is our response? Love the Lord back with good works. He will show you what He prepared for you to do. Walk with Him. Talk with Him. Read His Word. He raised you from the dead in order that He could be in a relationship with you. Enjoy!

40

Unity of the Spirit

**I therefore, a prisoner for the Lord, urge you to walk in a
manner worthy of the calling to which you have been called,
with all humility and gentleness, with patience, bearing
with one another in love, eager to maintain the unity of
the Spirit in the bond of peace. There is one body and one
Spirit—just as you were called to the one hope that belongs
to your call—one Lord, one faith, one baptism, one God and
Father of all, who is over all and through all and in all.**

EPHESIANS 4:1–6

What are you eager for right now? Would you consider making a list of those things that take center stage in your thought life? Would the unity of the Spirit make the list if you had a few extra pages to keep writing?

We give nodding agreement to passages like this all the time. When was the last time anyone preached on this and took any steps toward real unity? Paul supplies the argument for his appeal, noting that there is only One in whom we have faith, hope, and baptism. We keep nodding through the end of the passage because we know this is all true. And it would be easier to keep going in agreement without going back to see what we are supposed to be doing about unity.

We are to walk in humility, gentleness, and patience. Humility is not hard until the comparison to others enters our minds. Gentleness is easy all day long, until we run into difficult people. And patience is ours, until our goals are thwarted. Unfortunately, all of these commands are for us to exude as we interact and deal with people who are not likely to do us the same favor. The command, however, does not change because of our circumstances.

The calling you received is to walk in the extraordinary steps of Jesus, to bear with everyone in love, like He did, even to the point of laying down your life for them. You will know you are where He wants you to be when you sense an eagerness to put others first, in love.

41

How You Walk

**Look carefully then how you walk, not as unwise but as wise,
making the best use of the time, because the days are evil.
Therefore do not be foolish, but understand what the will
of the Lord is. And do not get drunk with wine, for that is
debauchery, but be filled with the Spirit, addressing one another
in psalms and hymns and spiritual songs, singing and making
melody to the Lord with your heart, giving thanks always and
for everything to God the Father in the name of our Lord Jesus
Christ, submitting to one another out of reverence for Christ.**

EPHESIANS 5:15–21

What word would you use to sum up the first sentence of this passage? Consider writing down some of those words. *Carefully* look at how you are walking, being wise, and making the most of your time. God is asking us to hear Him clearly and understand His will. To walk without understanding His will, He calls foolishness. Disciplined and diligent, come to Him.

If the second sentence in this passage does not resonate with you and describe your walk, can you identify the reason it does not? A heart submitted to the Lord Jesus Christ will be filled with the Spirit. It will give thanks and praise. It will sing and make a joyful noise to the Lord. And it will submit to one another in love. God's will is that your walk with Him would bear this kind of fruit. If you see that your walk is not bearing this kind of fruit, take that to God in humble confession. Ask Him to help you look carefully at your relationship with Him and adopt new reverence for Christ.

The time for bearing fruit is now. Make the most of your time and diligently pursue Him while you can. Ensure you understand His good, pleasing, and perfect will for your life.

42

Stand Firm

Finally, be strong in the Lord and in the strength of his might. Put on the whole armor of God, that you may be able to stand against the schemes of the devil. For we do not wrestle against flesh and blood, but against the rulers, against the authorities, against the cosmic powers over this present darkness, against the spiritual forces of evil in the heavenly places. Therefore take up the whole armor of God, that you may be able to withstand in the evil day, and having done all, to stand firm. Stand therefore, having fastened on the belt of truth, and having put on the breastplate of righteousness, and, as shoes for your feet, having put on the readiness given by the gospel of peace. In all circumstances take up the shield of faith, with which you can extinguish all the flaming darts of the evil one; and take the helmet of salvation, and the sword of the Spirit, which is the word of God, praying at all times in the Spirit, with all prayer and supplication. To that end, keep alert with all perseverance, making supplication for all the saints, and also for me, that words may be given to me in opening my mouth boldly to proclaim the mystery of the gospel, for which I am an ambassador in chains, that I may declare it boldly, as I ought to speak.

EPHESIANS 6:10–18

These are likely some very familiar words to you, as this is a popular passage in Christian circles: the whole armor of God. In the face of the familiar, let's not miss what should be obvious. The analogous description helps us appreciate spiritual terms, but we need not miss the point while stuck in the analogy. If you are not "strong in the Lord and in the strength of his might," maybe you missed the point.

The devil is going to scheme against you. The devil has cosmic, evil powers over this present darkness. The devil has weapons of evil, and he is warring against you and all that is good. The Lord, however, has commanded you to lean not on your own wisdom or powers in this struggle. He wants you to lean on Him. God will win this battle. Go with the winner.

To that winning conclusion, God has given us everything we need to be strong and courageous, standing firm in Him. He has provided His truth and His righteousness. Are you ready to proclaim the Gospel of peace? He has provided you with faith, salvation, and the Holy Spirit—the Word of God. With these gifts in and on your mind, are you constant in prayer?

Are you alert with perseverance, seeking Him who has ordained victory in this battle?

Don't miss the battle fiddling with the equipment. Put it on, and let's get to work.

43

Worthy Manner

Only let your manner of life be worthy of the gospel of Christ, so that whether I come and see you or am absent, I may hear of you that you are standing firm in one spirit, with one mind striving side by side for the faith of the gospel, and not frightened in anything by your opponents. This is a clear sign to them of their destruction, but of your salvation, and that from God. For it has been granted to you that for the sake of Christ you should not only believe in him but also suffer for his sake, engaged in the same conflict that you saw I had and now hear that I still have.

PHILIPPIANS 1:27–30

Are you living life in a manner worthy of the Gospel of Jesus Christ? You should be. Living your life as a gift back to the One who gave you life is the only way to love Him back. Living in obedience to Jesus is how we demonstrate that we love Him. Please don't think that you cannot live your life in a worthy manner. The perfectionist will look to change the words or the meaning. We should look to move toward the right direction and let go of perfection.

Standing firm in the Spirit is a good test of direction. Striving side by side for the faith of the Gospel—is this where you find yourself currently? Are you in the trenches with other believers contending for the faith of the Gospel? It's hard to do phoning it in from the couch.

Another good test of direction is to gauge what makes us fearful. Does sharing your faith energize you, or does the thought of telling someone else about your faith bring fear? Consider writing out what brings you fear. These things are not of the Lord. Pray over these things and ask that God would replace them with confidence.

Suffering for the sake of Christ seems to run concurrent with walking in faithful obedience to Him. Some will confuse the natural consequences of bad decisions with suffering for Christ. They are not the same. Bad decisions will tend to be repeated by bad decision makers. Suffering for Christ will embolden the believer, enhance their faith, and draw them to an even closer walk with their Savior.

This is walking in a manner worthy of the Gospel of Christ. How is your walk?

44

Upward Call

Not that I have already obtained this or am already perfect, but I press on to make it my own, because Christ Jesus has made me his own. Brothers, I do not consider that I have made it my own. But one thing I do: forgetting what lies behind and straining forward to what lies ahead, I press on toward the goal for the prize of the upward call of God in Christ Jesus. Let those of us who are mature think this way, and if in anything you think otherwise, God will reveal that also to you. Only let us hold true to what we have attained.

PHILIPPIANS 3:12–16

Paul is describing the earthly struggle of all followers of Jesus Christ. We have been bought and paid for by a Holy God, through the blood sacrifice of His Only Son. We are called, by the One who is perfect, to be perfect. It is at once a position and a plan. We are perfect in Christ, and yet perfection eludes us in practice. We are still on the path of perfection following in the direction of Perfection.

This is the upward call of God in Jesus Christ. Paul confesses that he has not attained perfection either. He does, however, give two mile-markers to check for as we head toward Perfection. The first is to forget what lies behind. There is no need for baggage in the direction of Perfection. Sins and mistakes that have been dealt with properly can be cut from your pack. You can move forward freely without continually dealing with what lies behind. If it helps, try writing down those things from your past that are weighing you down. Pray over that list and give it to Jesus.

The second marker Paul describes is one of diligence. Paul describes his spiritual walk as *straining forward.* How would you describe your walk with Christ? Comfortable? Stand-still? Paul's strain is forward toward the goal. Jesus is calling us up the road toward Perfection, Himself. This is the prize. An eternal relationship with Jesus is the road to Perfection.

Press on, like Paul, toward Jesus Himself.

45

Contentment

**I rejoiced in the Lord greatly that now at length you have
revived your concern for me. You were indeed concerned for
me, but you had no opportunity. Not that I am speaking of
being in need, for I have learned in whatever situation I am
to be content. I know how to be brought low, and I know how
to abound. In any and every circumstance, I have learned
the secret of facing plenty and hunger, abundance and need.
I can do all things through him who strengthens me.**

PHILIPPIANS 4:10–13

Most of the time, this passage is quoted because of the wonderful conclusion that we can do anything and everything through Christ who gives us strength. With that conclusion in hand, we set out to see that our will is done, with the nod to Christ, who is going to give us strength for our task.

Paul, however, is describing how Jesus has provided for him in his varying circumstances and allowed him to be content, regardless of the circumstances. Paul has learned the secret of contentment whether he is hungry or full, being stoned or receiving new believers, having everything or having nothing. What is your level of contentment? What would it take to bring you the contentment you are seeking?

I asked my girlfriend what it would take to make her happy. She replied that she was already happy. I married her! Contentment is only found in Jesus. No amount of money, success, or fame will fill the void designed to be filled by the Lord. If you are discontent, know that you are looking for contentment in the wrong places. Those things will never bring you to the point that you will say you are now content.

Many today will quote this verse in their own effort to claim those things they think will get them to a point of contentedness. The secret is hiding in plain sight. Jesus is the answer. If you have been expecting contentment based on your changing circumstances, expect to be disappointed. Lean into Jesus for an eternity of contentment.

46

New Self

**If then you have been raised with Christ, seek the things that
are above, where Christ is, seated at the right hand of God. Set
your minds on things that are above, not on things that are on
earth. For you have died, and your life is hidden with Christ in
God. When Christ who is your life appears, then you also will
appear with him in glory. Put to death therefore what is earthly
in you: sexual immorality, impurity, passion, evil desire, and
covetousness, which is idolatry. On account of these the wrath
of God is coming. In these you too once walked, when you were
living in them. But now you must put them all away: anger,
wrath, malice, slander, and obscene talk from your mouth.
Do not lie to one another, seeing that you have put off the old
self with its practices and have put on the new self, which is
being renewed in knowledge after the image of its creator.**

COLOSSIANS 3:1–10

What a wonderful contrast: raised from the dead with Christ, setting our
minds on things above, yet still having to kill what remains of our old self.
If Paul's list hits too close to home, and you see in yourself these things that
should not be in the life of one hidden in Christ, you know what to do. The
antidote to earthly, unspiritual life, is all about where you fix your gaze.
Your mind is on the things of this earth, and you are reaping what is sown
in your mind. Change your focus and set your gaze on things above: your
God and your Savior.

This is a continual process. As you grow and mature in your faith,
the Lord will make you more aware of earthly sin. Don't beat yourself up.
Put the sin out of your life and refix your mind on Him. The wrath of
God is coming. Continue putting to death earthly attributes and trust that
your Savior will appear and hide you with Himself. You have been raised
with Christ. Let's start acting like it. Shake off the dust of this world and
continue the process of putting on your new self—your identity in Jesus
Christ. You are being renewed in the knowledge of Christ.

47

God's Will

Rejoice always, pray without ceasing, give thanks in all circumstances; for this is the will of God in Christ Jesus for you.

1 THESSALONIANS 5:16–18

God's will for you in Christ Jesus is very clear. How often do we allow indecisiveness or inaction to have their way in the inability to discern God's will? His will has been made crystal clear. Do we tend to forego this simple aspect of His will, in search of new and different aspects of what His will might be in our lives?

The truth is, when we are busy doing the part of His will that we know to do, the rest becomes clear as well. If you are actively rejoicing, praying, and giving thanks to Him, He will speak in a voice that you will hear and understand. When we occupy ourselves with the things of this earth, the chorus in our ears will drown out the song of the Savior.

We are to rejoice always, so there is not a time to cease rejoicing. This is the attitude of a heart consumed with the fact you have been saved by faith, through grace, undeservedly—it will be consumed with rejoicing. Consider making some notes about the many things you should be rejoicing over today. Make a plan to rejoice. Make a plan to be *intentional* about rejoicing, *always*.

Prayer is conversation with the Lord. The conversation should never stop. Whether you are busy with your hands or sitting at a computer all day, the Lord is with you. He wants to hear from you. Practice His presence. Speak truth in Scripture to Him. Tell Him your thoughts. Ask for His guidance.

God's will for you is that you give thanks, regardless of your circumstances. There is no free pass for not being thankful. You were made alive in Christ while you were dead in sin. Therefore, you have everything to be thankful for, from now on, into the glorious eternity you have been given.

48

Good Challenge

Have nothing to do with irreverent, silly myths. Rather train yourself for godliness; for while bodily training is of some value, godliness is of value in every way, as it holds promise for the present life and also for the life to come.

1 TIMOTHY 4:7–8

Becoming like Jesus in our thoughts and our actions should be our goal. Scripture reminds us that this is more than just a worthy goal; God says to *do it*. Godliness will follow us from this life into the life that is to come. There is great value in being Christlike, both now and in eternity. How often do we acknowledge this passage, agree with the tenets, and then go back to whatever we were doing?

The Bible says *train yourself* to be godly. How will you go about training yourself to be godly? How do you go about training yourself in other worldly pursuits? Do you get up early to train? Utilize a training partner or a training plan/app? Take a class? Read a good book? You will want support and challenge in the pursuit of godliness, so I would recommend all of the above activities. We do these things in the pursuit of godly perfection. The test is direction. Activity in pursuit of Jesus is the right direction.

Consider writing out a simple plan to move yourself in the direction of godliness. Regardless of your current level, we can all benefit from additional, intentional training toward godliness. If you have already achieved perfection in godliness, you can disregard this passage. The rest of us have to take this passage seriously and get busy with the training. Can we start today, now?

If you suspect that there are areas in your life that are not holy, make a confession of those things. Write them down and turn them over to a Holy God. Repentance is the business of a sober-minded follower of Jesus Christ. Then, prepare your mind for action and wait to hear from your Savior regarding what you are to do next.

Pray for a partner in challenging you to greater godliness, someone who will help with accountability. Would you also be that accountability and challenge for someone who is praying for partnership in pursuing godliness?

49

Take Hold

But godliness with contentment is great gain, for we brought nothing into the world, and we cannot take anything out of the world. But if we have food and clothing, with these we will be content. But those who desire to be rich fall into temptation, into a snare, into many senseless and harmful desires that plunge people into ruin and destruction. For the love of money is a root of all kinds of evils. It is through this craving that some have wandered away from the faith and pierced themselves with many pangs. But as for you, O man of God, flee these things. Pursue righteousness, godliness, faith, love, steadfastness, gentleness. Fight the good fight of the faith. Take hold of the eternal life to which you were called and about which you made the good confession in the presence of many witnesses.

1 TIMOTHY 6:6–12

We have heard it said that money is the root of all evil. Scripture does not echo that claim. Read it closely and look at different translations. In this passage, Paul is advising Timothy of two truths, or two paths you can take in life. Neither path promises wealth, and neither path includes the need to necessarily forego wealth. Money and wealth are provisions of the Lord for which we are 100 percent accountable. He may choose to make that provision to you, and He may not. In the end, you don't take your wealth with you.

Consider making a side-by-side list of what Scripture actually says here about the two paths Paul is describing. One path is of those who are content with food and clothing alone. On this path is righteousness, godliness, and so on. The alternate path is one where the heart's desire is for riches. The love of money drives their thoughts and actions. Their level of contentment is dependent on circumstances, which are measured by possessions and the accumulation of wealth.

If you are consumed with fighting the good fight of faith, you are on the right path. Eternal life is yours already, and death is merely a change of state from the physical to the spiritual. If, however, your grip is on the things of this world, how are you to also take hold of eternal life?

We all tend to want more. The new car is only new for so long before we want a newer, new car, a slightly larger house, on a better lot, in a better neighborhood. Make those thoughts and desires answer to Jesus. Look to the needs of others when tempted to think of more for yourself. This is fighting the good fight, making every thought captive to Christ. How is your fight looking?

50

Discipline

Therefore, since we are surrounded by so great a cloud of witnesses, let us also lay aside every weight, and sin which clings so closely, and let us run with endurance the race that is set before us, looking to Jesus, the founder and perfecter of our faith, who for the joy that was set before him endured the cross, despising the shame, and is seated at the right hand of the throne of God. Consider him who endured from sinners such hostility against himself, so that you may not grow weary or fainthearted. In your struggle against sin you have not yet resisted to the point of shedding your blood. And have you forgotten the exhortation that addresses you as sons? "My son, do not regard lightly the discipline of the Lord, nor be weary when reproved by him. For the Lord disciplines the one he loves, and chastises every son whom he receives." It is for discipline that you have to endure. God is treating you as sons. For what son is there whom his father does not discipline? If you are left without discipline, in which all have participated, then you are illegitimate children and not sons. Besides this, we have had earthly fathers who disciplined us and we respected them. Shall we not much more be subject to the Father of spirits and live? For they disciplined us for a short time as it seemed best to them, but he disciplines us for our good, that we may share his holiness. For the moment all discipline seems painful rather than pleasant, but later it yields the peaceful fruit of righteousness to those who have been trained by it.

HEBREWS 12:1–11

How many examples do we need before we believe and submit to the Lord and His discipline? How long will we continue to fight and resist being trained by the very trials the Lord intends to use for our good and His glory? Consider making an outline of this passage for yourself. Do you see a new trend emerge from the passage? If you read the last sentence of the passage first and then read backwards to the top, does the familiar passage become unfamiliar but now clear?

Sin wants to cling closely to you. Shake it off! Shake harder! Look to Jesus in your sufferings, persevering, and being trained in the process. The Triune God of the Bible loves you and calls you a son. As a child, we are called to endure His discipline, not avoid or begrudge it. This week, determine that you will see your own sin as evil and the hardships you encounter as an opportunity for a deeper relationship with your Savior.

51

Various Trials

Count it all joy, my brothers, when you meet trials of various kinds, for you know that the testing of your faith produces steadfastness. And let steadfastness have its full effect, that you may be perfect and complete, lacking in nothing. If any of you lacks wisdom, let him ask God, who gives generously to all without reproach, and it will be given him. But let him ask in faith, with no doubting, for the one who doubts is like a wave of the sea that is driven and tossed by the wind. For that person must not suppose that he will receive anything from the Lord; he is a double-minded man, unstable in all his ways.

JAMES 1:2–8

What effect do trials have on you in your life? Do you despise hardships and trials? Scripture says to count it all *joy*. Really? Yes, really. Negative reactions to the trials of life suggest that either you or the world is in charge. God claims that He created the world and everything in it. God says He is in charge. How you face trials, see trials, and endure them is a reflection of what you believe about who is in charge. Your faith is being tested.

If you see that trials do not typically prompt the right response, make this a subject of prayer. Ask the Lord for a fresh perspective on trials.

> "Lord, would you give me a right and joyful perspective
> on the trials of life?"

One by one, trials will come. When we adopt the right attitude about these trials and hardships, we will learn to see them differently. We *can* learn to appreciate the testing of our faith. The testing proves our faith genuine and creates steadfastness or faith muscles.

Make doing what is right, with joy, your intentional priority this week. Ask the Lord to make clear to you what you are hearing, seeing, and reading so that you may incorporate these things into action despite the distracting trials. Maybe this time that passage is for *you* to hear and deal with, not just the other people in the room. Maybe you need to read the Bible standing in front of a mirror so you can look and see to whom to apply that difficult passage.

God's Word is a stumbling block to the unwise. You are wise when you approach the Word, knowing God will instruct you in the ways of wisdom as you read, and put what you are reading into action.

There is great wisdom is seeing things with godly perspective. Count the trials of life as all joy and escape the negativity of a worldly perspective.

52

Abide in Him

My little children, I am writing these things to you so that you may not sin. But if anyone does sin, we have an advocate with the Father, Jesus Christ the righteous. He is the propitiation for our sins, and not for ours only but also for the sins of the whole world. And by this we know that we have come to know him, if we keep his commandments. Whoever says "I know him" but does not keep his commandments is a liar, and the truth is not in him, but whoever keeps his word, in him truly the love of God is perfected. By this we may know that we are in him: whoever says he abides in him ought to walk in the same way in which he walked.

1 JOHN 2:1–6

Jesus Christ is our righteous advocate. There is no other name by which we will be saved. Have we really grasped the truth and gravity of this passage? If so, our lives will reflect that truth in keeping His commands.

Jesus is the appeasement for God's wrath. He is the only satisfaction for a debt we incurred and could never repay. Every knee will bow, and every tongue will confess Jesus as Lord. Many will invoke His name on the day of judgment. Few will claim to know Him and still escape condemnation. That road is narrow, and words will be of little value. Knowing Jesus means obeying Jesus. The love of God is perfected in a relationship with His Son, Jesus Christ.

Do you know someone who knows the facts about Jesus but does not *know* Him? Do you love that person like Jesus? Are you willing to jump the fence and tell your neighbor the truth about a saving relationship with the Lord Jesus Christ?

Jesus desires to be an advocate on our behalf. The price for your eternal freedom has already been paid. A relationship with the advocate, the righteous Lord, is the entryway to eternal life. Do you love the Lord and your neighbor enough to introduce them?

Abiding in Christ, submitting to Him in love and faithfulness, is where you should strive to be found. When we are walking so closely with the Lord that we cast only one shadow, then and only then can we be sure to hear and understand where He directs us to go. Your own wisdom, your own understanding will fail you. Trust in Jesus with your whole heart. Lean into Him for understanding beyond your own wisdom and experience. He will guide you in the way you should go. Peace will be added to your walk, and you can be assured of His perfect will.

Who will you introduce your Savior to this week?

Afterword

What now? I trust that you are like a sharp knife—honed on both edges and ready to be made useful by the Lord. God knows what to do when we are prepared. Opportunities of all kinds were prepared for us long before we were born:

For we are his workmanship, created in Christ Jesus for good works, which God prepared beforehand, that we should walk in them.

EPHESIANS 2:10

When athletes have put in the time and effort to be strong and fast, and to be good at their sport, they look for opportunities to get in the game. Are you looking for opportunities to engage in the work of the Lord? Moving in the right direction (letting go of perfection), the Lord will use you to advance His kingdom. Continue praying for your role and His will to be done. The world needs you to be salt and light—support and challenge.

Go show the world the love of Jesus Christ.

Acknowledgments

Thank you to my bride and best friend, Sandra. She is more than a Proverbs 31 wife. Thank you for the support and challenge needed to do this right. You put aside your own writing at times to help me with mine. Thank you for your needed editing and constant encouragement. You are beautiful inside and out. The Lord has over-blessed me with you.

Dr. Jason Jarvis read and offered valuable insight into each page. Thank you, brother, for your example of servant leadership, deep friendship, and followership of Jesus. You have an amazing eye for detail and a gift for support and challenge. No wonder the Lord saw fit to use you as a pastor. Thank you for all your help with my writing projects. "No Reserve, No Retreat, No Regret."

About the Author

Photo by Chris Germain at genesismediasolutions.com

Ken Valentine retired from the United States Secret Service in 2020 as the Special Agent in Charge of the Dignitary Protective Division in the Office of Protective Operations. His career on the Presidential Protective Detail spanned ten years and three presidencies, during which he was in charge of White House access controls and worldwide operational security. He and Sandra have been married thirty-plus years and have five amazing children.

Since his retirement from the Secret Service, Ken has served on the board of directors at The National Center for Missing and Exploited Children where he chairs the Operations & Law Enforcement Committee. He is a certified leadership trainer through Pointman Leadership Institute, teaches a group class at The Church at Brook Hills, and serves on the board of directors at The WellHouse, a home for human trafficking victims. He is on the board of advisors for Base Molecular Resonance Technologies (www.BMRT.io) looking for early detection of unwanted substances like weapons, cancer, and illegal drugs.

Ken is the author of *Cheating Death*, widely available from Post Hill Press. Ken holds an undergraduate degree from Purdue University, a law degree from Mississippi College, and leadership training certifications from Harvard, Johns Hopkins, and American Universities. Ken is available for speaking and leadership consulting through www.KennethValentine.com.